Downsizing

Ultimate Guide On How To Change Your Life With A Minimalistic Approach By Organizing

(Creative Ways To Simplify Your Life)

Sharon Bryant

Published By **Simon Dough**

Sharon Bryant

All Rights Reserved

Downsizing: Ultimate Guide On How To Change Your Life With A Minimalistic Approach By Organizing (Creative Ways To Simplify Your Life)

ISBN 978-1-77485-930-8

No part of this guidebook shall be reproduced in any form without permission in writing from the publisher except in the case of brief quotations embodied in critical articles or reviews.

Legal & Disclaimer

The information contained in this ebook is not designed to replace or take the place of any form of medicine or professional medical advice. The information in this ebook has been provided for educational & entertainment purposes only.

The information contained in this book has been compiled from sources deemed reliable, and it is accurate to the best of the Author's knowledge; however, the Author cannot guarantee its accuracy and validity and cannot be held liable for any errors or omissions. Changes are periodically made to this book. You must consult your doctor or get professional medical advice before using any of the suggested remedies, techniques, or information in this book.

Upon using the information contained in this book, you agree to hold harmless the Author from and against any damages, costs, and expenses, including any legal fees potentially resulting from the application of any of the information provided by this guide. This disclaimer applies to any damages or injury caused by the use and application, whether directly or indirectly, of any advice or information presented, whether for breach of contract, tort, negligence, personal injury, criminal intent, or under any other cause of action.

You agree to accept all risks of using the information presented inside this book. You need to consult a professional medical practitioner in order to ensure you are both able and healthy enough to participate in this program.

Table of Contents

Chapter 1: What Is Too Much In Life? 1

Chapter 2: Make A Plan! 3

Chapter 3: Live With Less 8

Chapter 5: Downsizing Method.............. 22

Chapter 6: Effective Tips To Keep Your Home Neat And Tidy All Year 33

Chapter 7: Five Signs To Make Your Life More Simple 36

Chapter 8: The Next Steps...................... 41

Chapter 9: Preventing Future Clutter 50

Chapter 10: Junk The Junk Warmer 53

Chapter 11: Start Early 61

Chapter 12: Simplify Your Life With Contentment 68

Chapter 13: Make Gratitude A Discipline 74

Chapter 14: Accept The Fact That You Will Always Need Bills To Pay........................ 77

Chapter 15: Emotionally Dealing A Minimalist Life Style 88

Chapter 16: Do The Math 96

Chapter 17: Minimalism in relation to Consumerism 100

Chapter 18: Minimalism in Your Daily Life 120

Chapter 19: Mindset Changes, Finding Balance 132

Chapter 20: How to Apply Your Life Gradually 152

Chapter 1: What Is Too Much In Life?

Is it not true that the society values happiness more than how much money? I hate the idea that success is based on how much I own. Although it may be tempting to own all the latest gadgets and every other possible thing, is it really worth the effort? There is no amount of activity or possession that can satisfy your need to succeed.

Every person has a different definition of success. Certain people might be more successful if they have more. Human nature doesn't require excess. All things are not luxury. We all have basic needs. When we transform our luxuries into necessities, we can become unhappy.

I have taken stock of my life and found that removing unnecessary things makes me happier. I'm not worried about getting more. What I have is enough. It was a relief to be able to accept that mentality. I didn't feel I had to do everything just to reach a goal.

Let's see how you do. Do you ever feel overwhelmed by the thought of all that is required to maintain what little you have? You need to take a closer look at your daily life. Are you trying to keep your excesses under control? Do you have things you can live with? If the answer to any questions is "yes", I encourage you not to hesitate to read this book. You will be able to see what is actually a need, and what is just a luxury. You may be surprised at the things you find about yourself.

I recommend that you continue reading if you want to simplify and streamline your life. I will share some tips and tricks in this book to help you reduce your stress levels so that you can truly enjoy what you have. You may discover that the simple life is your best option and you'll love it just as much as I do.

Chapter 2: Make A Plan!

There is no way to move in 8 working days without a plan.

We'll start by doing this. Take a look at the time you have and determine which rooms you must complete.

Spend some time in previously unexplored areas such as heavy storage spaces. Before proceeding with downsizing, sorting, and the like, read Chapter 4.

It's also a good idea to find out who can assist you. Get help if your schedule is tight and you don't have time to do it all yourself.

If you're tech-savvy and want to get your friends involved, you can send texts, emails, or phone calls.

Here's where you will get the most help:

You should go through large spaces like attic or basement.

Pack obvious items (kitchen stuffs, pantry items, trinkets or household items).

Laden the truck

The old place should be cleaned

Clean the new place because you know it hasn't been done enough.

Unloading the truck

Part A: The attic or basement

These are the areas you should start working on before you move. Ask for help from your neighbors, friends, and family.

The biggest obstacle when you want to downsize is your mind.

You don't have to downsize if clutter is not an issue and/or you don't mind packing this stuff quickly.

You must have a positive attitude regardless of what is happening.

It is likely that you will have to get rid off a lot.

It is also worth throwing away if it was not easily accessible when you needed it.

Consider it this way. It's beautiful china that you have, but you can't get it out of your home because it's too complicated. Give it to someone in your family.

This tent might be useful if you ever want to go camping. You haven't been camping in 10 years. You should get rid of it.

You should also consider how much storage you need in the new area.

Are you sure there is enough room? You don't have to move it if you feel it will waste your energy.

Part B: Bedrooms

These should be packed as soon as possible.

Take out clothing, bedding, and everyday necessities. Everything else should go in a separate box

Part C: Living Room

Take everything, except the TV.

To unwind, you'll need to have a few minutes at the end.

Part D: Kitchen

It is important to have everything, except the essentials.

I am referring to 1 frying skillet (woks can be used to cook pasta), 1 baking pan, utensils, and other basic kitchen items.

Do not keep too many kitchen tools or different pots and saucepans. You won't have time to cook anyway.

Paper plates can be purchased for the last day of cooking.

Order pizzas and other foods. It takes no time to prepare, just like I said. PB&J must be a part of your daily diet!

You should always have scissors, scissors, or more scissors on hand for move-IN.

Part E: Office/Miscrooms

If you do not need it right away, don't pack it. End of story.

Do not pack anything that is required paperwork, or a house you're selling.

Chapter 3: Live With Less

This chapter is directly linked to the previous. Simple tastes can lead to a satisfaction with getting enough (in quantities).

This part doesn't need to be complicated. Living with less means not choosing to be average, not reaching your full potential, and not fighting for what's rightfully yours. It is simply about having enough and not accumulating too much. Being able to possess material things is not enough to live up your full potential.

Now let's return to the point. Many house organizers advise that you practice the "one in and one out" rule. This means that every new item that is purchased, another belonging of yours should be disposed. Therefore, if you decide to buy a new T-shirt, choose one from your wardrobe that you will give away, toss out, or place in the Goodwill pile.

It is possible to reduce the number of your material possessions by using the "one-in, one-out" rule. What if there are so many things you already own? The following steps will help to reduce your overflow and teach you how to live with fewer.

Take care of the house

Yes, of course! Grab your garbage bags, cleaning supplies and boxes and get ready for some serious sweat!

Start in one space and work your way to the next. Use bags to separate trash, Goodwill, storage and other items. When sorting your possessions, use the simplicity principle. Don't keep things that you no longer use or don't need. For later, you can put away items that are rarely used but still in good condition. Only keep in storage seasonal items like winter clothes, sports equipment, and other clothing.

Here's a handy checklist to help you decide what items to throw away.

Charity: Donate

Don't forget those clothes or other items you left behind. It is a smart idea to either donate them or give them away. Although it may be hard to part with things you have, keeping them will only increase your closet space. It is easier to give them away to those who are more likely to use them. They'll be used more often and will serve their purposes better than sitting in a pile of dust.

You won't waste money if you give to charity. Giving to charity will allow you to assist people in need. This is a good reason to make a habit of cleaning out your closets every now and again.

Make cleaning a habit

This is an important step in maintaining a clutter-free home. People don't often realize the amount of trash they keep around until they begin accumulating inside drawers and pockets.

Many people keep receipts, for various reasons. A receipt can be inserted in your planner, but it is still tidy. You will soon start to see clutter when you have 10 or more slips of paper. The same holds true for magazines and newspapers, subscription mails as well as emails, coupons, and clothes.

You should make it a habit of keeping receipts, doodle notes and other paperwork in one location. Once you've completed your monthly expenses or obtained the information you require, discard them. Save room for the next months receipts and doodles, and do the same at month's end.

Subscriptions, magazines and newspapers can be thrown out on a quarterly base. Because we don't want to throw away these things, they end up being stockpiled. After all, you did pay for them. You can enjoy this for up to 3 months. After that, they should be thrown away.

**Note that it is better to limit your subscriptions solely to one or a couple magazines. Subscriptions can be canceled if possible. Simply go to the store and buy the issue you are most interested in. You can even save money by doing this.

Here are some tips for how to clear clutter and make your home more organized.

Sort your mail while you are still outside near the mailbox. If mail arrives through your apartment's mailbox, you can stand in front of a trash bin to sort them. Get rid of anything you aren't interested in.

Grab anything that's not needed.

Do 10 minutes of tidying up each morning after the children go to school and at night after they have gone to bed. This is much more efficient than waiting for the weekend to tidy up and spending hours cleaning.

Your clothes should go to the hamper upon your return from work or hang on the back wall.

You can use the hanger to store jackets or coats.

You shouldn't take trash home. Don't take more than you can drink.

You should always order Chinese from the box. Do not use sauces or any other food that would saturate your carton.

You can start folding your laundry while you wait for the next batch to dry in the dryer.

Keep toddlers under control in one or two rooms of your house.

For little ones, you can create "bring us" games and other similar games that will get them to help clean up after themselves.

Give specific purposes for open surfaces. Examples: books on bedside table, suitcase on hallway table, laptop, schoolbooks, and cookie jar on kitchen counter. Mail on low shelves.

Make sure you have a place to store your recyclables. This box can hold newspapers, boxes, plastic containers, and any other material that can be used for arts, crafts, and the like.

The contents of the recyclables container can be used. Toss them out if they start filling up.

Designate one kitchen drawer "junk drawer". This drawer can be used for random items like rubber bands or screws, as well as knobs, knobs, and empty spices bottles.

Make sure you only purchase the amount that is necessary. This applies to food, clothing, home maintenance, and repair materials, etc. Extras will most likely end up as clutter.

Oprah.com provides a simplified version.

These rules will help keep your home orderly and clean. You will not become a compulsive hoarder.

Grab your phone camera, and go through every room in your house. Take as many "before" photos as you can of each area.

When you are done with each space, go through it and take a "after" photograph.

It can be very motivating to look at the work you have completed after each task is complete and then revisit these photos when you feel low or discouraged.

You'll soon have less to do and your motivation for doing so will increase.

Desks, closets and pantry are all areas to be photographed. Don't be afraid to take as many pictures as you need in order to document your task.

Sorting: Keepers and Losers

Once you have made the major decision to decide what to keep and discard, the real work begins.

It is sad that only 80% are used. American adults spend over 30 minutes per day just searching for things. Millions of people suffer from compulsive hoarding.

As you go through a box or drawer, a closet, or room, ask yourself the following questions.

Do I know where the item is located? Surprisingly enough, many objects we hold on to don't know their true identity. It doesn't matter if the item isn't yours, just get rid of it.

A second obvious problem is if the item actually works. You should throw away any part that is broken or not functioning properly.

How often do your use this item? It is best to dispose of the item that you haven't used in the past year.

Is the item being kept for sentimental purposes? Are you keeping it because it is a memento of someone, a place or a time? These are the hardest to make a decision on. It is best to let these items go as soon as possible. A great way to let go of an item is to take a photo of it that reminds you of a particular time or place. You can then keep that memory as a memento instead of the actual item. That way, you will always have the memories and reminders of those special moments without having to store or maintain the item.

Is the item bulky or large? If the item is excessively large or heavy, it should be thrown out. Because space and storage are scarce, you should look at bulky or large objects with a fresh perspective. Is this worth the space it takes up in my new home? Is there a way to get a smaller or more efficient version of this item?

It will be put in my new, de-cluttered space. As far as storage, make sure you have a plan. It must be accessible easily, if it's worth keeping.

It is difficult and frustrating to make these choices. If you're doing this yourself, take your own time and limit your decision making sessions to two hours. Do not save any money that you don't believe is useful, or worth the effort.

Don't hesitate to ask for help or hire professionals to help you sell your unwanted items. You should only take what you can live without. Shut the door, box or cabinet. It is important to not look back. This will allow you to move on to a better, less burdened lifestyle.

With a little planning, you can make a list with "no-brainers" items that you can give up.

All paperwork, bills, and bank statements can now be handled online. All this can be done online. All paper is now redundant.

CD's & DVD's - They are all available on cable and online streaming. You don't need boxes, cases or shelving anymore for these old technologies.

To scan and convert any paperwork to PDF, hire an archiving provider. These services can convert thousands of documents to PDF files in no time.

Toss the maps! No more maps! Google and Apple Maps are accessible online or on any Smartphone. They are continually updated.

Sort through all of your cabinets, refrigerators, and freezer and toss anything that is past its expiration date. It's unlikely that you will ever eat it.

Get rid your old foreign currency. If you're like most people you have a lot of foreign currency and small bills. It doesn't amount to much and you won't ever spend it so why not give it away?

This brings us to the topic of grandkids. Toys such as plush toys and stuffed animals must be thrown out. Toss them or throw them out, but they won't last long and can't be forgotten.

Check your medicine box and toss any expired items or tooth brushes that you haven't used within the last 6 months.

It is usually a good idea not to keep any cables or wires in your home. You won't use these wires again thanks to wireless technology. It is difficult to match the right piece with an AC plug adapter. They are heavy, bulky, and cumbersome. If you don't know the origin of each plug or where it belongs, throw them away. These wires are available on Amazon within one day and very cheap if they become necessary.

Finally, get rid any Yellow Pages, phone directories, or phone books you might have stored in your garage. These obsolete, and everything you'll need on any Smartphone is accessible in an instant, are they?

Discover "Decluttr".

A new app can help you rid your home of unwanted books and dvds, Blu-Rays or games.

You can start downsizing by getting rid of many of these items.

A new App, "Decluttr," is available for download on your Smartphone and computer.

It's easy to get started. All you have to do is scan the barcodes from any books or dvds you don't want and they will give you a value price.

Be careful not to get excited. You may find your books and CDs less valuable than you think. Decluttr can help you sell them on Ebay and other auction sites.

Decluttr is able to pay shipping costs for your items, and you will be paid the next day. There are no fees for selling or auction and your old media can be recycled instead of being thrown in a landfill. They even earn you a few dollars.

If they don't recognize you bar code number then it is not worth anything and you can throw it out as having no monetary value.

This is a quick, easy and clean way to unload bulky items by one source. It is easy and fun!

Chapter 5: Downsizing Method

This chapter will focus on the most essential and basic parts of your daily life, and how they can be reduced. Although our lives are different, everyone does the same things. These tips can help you organize your personal and professional life in a way you never thought possible, regardless of your lifestyle. Don't forget that not all things have to be downsized. It is likely that you are perfectly content with how you are doing in at least one aspect. If that happens, you can take a moment of self-congratulation.

Minimalist living is best when you reduce your belongings. Don't let your belongings go without giving thought to how they might impact you. Although minimalists do it differently, many people end up downsizing their possessions. The common theme is to get rid the stuff you don't use and keep the items you do. I would also suggest that you keep some items you don't need, but that you truly love and have great sentimental value. You can consider it a form need if you are deeply attached. For instance, very few minimalists would recommend that you get rid a pet of ten year because it is not contributing to your rent and is a nuisance to the house.

But how do you choose which things to keep and which to dispose of? Some say to keep anything you don't use frequently in storage. After a month, if you can't recall what you have put away, that's an indication you don't require them and you should get rid. Others recommend keeping them in storage for a year. If they don't serve any purpose, you can dispose of them. Keep everything you don't need. Wait a while until you see what you do miss. Put these items in your attic, garage, or basement and forget about it for a few days. The item can be evicted if you go back into the attic or garage and discover that you totally forgot about it. It's fairly simple to figure out what you need and not. You don't need to keep any item for a specific time in the future. Instead, you can look back at the history. There are items that you can simply decide to get rid of and free up space. A piano you don't know how to play should be sold. It's best to get rid of a Halloween costume you haven't worn in at least five years. These are not difficult decisions. You have to make hard choices when you have something that's really handy, even if it's not used often. These tools are tools. If you don't use a tool in a while, and it doesn't take up any space, you can keep it. If the tool takes up space or is a clutter, it should be sold or given away. Items that hold sentimental value are another difficult decision. You can't convince yourself to get rid of something if it has sentimental value. However, there are some things that will not only clutter your home but also clutter your mind. A gift from your first boyfriend, who you have no idea of where he's at or what he does, is a waste both physically and emotionally. These are the things you should get rid of.

After getting rid off a lot of clutter, you may feel as though you have too much space. If your house starts to echo when you return home, this is a sign that it is too big. It's easy to find a smaller home. Many people do not want to move. It can feel like they're stuck in their own world and cannot move to another place. Consider it an adventure. It is a chance to discover new possibilities and explore new things. It should be enjoyable

Minimize your commitments. Stress is easiest when you have no time to worry or worry. Many people think being busy means being productive and valuable. That is, having a lifestyle. Yes, it is about having a quality life. Are you happy with your life? Do you feel like you are stuck, or going nowhere quickly? If you don't feel like you are in a good spot, it is time to reevaluate your options.

What are the signs of an overabundance in commitments? It could be your job, your family, or both. It is not a good idea to stay in one job for too long. It's not always your fault that your job is so stressful. There are many things you can do to improve your job. It could be that the job is too stressful or that your boss is simply difficult. This is where switching jobs can help. Good pay is great, but you might consider switching to a job that offers more freedom and more time. You will be amazed at the benefits that two extra hours of sleep can bring. While you can't reduce the family size, if you're a breadwinner for an extended family, then you might want teach your family to fish. You may also consider hiring them to do certain tasks for you, and then paying them. This won't change much, but it does help. You must learn to say "no" and not accept it as a given. Be aware that not everything is easy. You can't meet all their needs. In other circumstances, it's your attention and time that is important. This time can be fun and enjoyable. But, if it makes you tired or leaves you feeling exhausted, then you should consider ways to reduce stress. Humans can be very adaptable. You will find they adapt and find other ways to get the items they need.

Negative attitudes can be minimized. Everybody has weaknesses. While some may be harmful to others, many are also detrimental to us. Anger, envy, and greed are just a few of the deadly sins. You can change them by internalizing them.

Do you have a quick fuse? Don't get mad at others. Accept situations you don't like and react rationally. Being able to shed your top is not always a positive trait. It will only cause you to be angry again or make you remorseful about what you did.

Envy is even more pervasive since most envious people won't admit to being envious to anyone. It is a poisonous emotion that can destroy one's happiness. It's when you feel unhappy because of someone else's happiness. Emotional baggage such as envy should be left behind. You'll feel many times more free if you can get rid of envy. It can make you feel unnecessarily anxious and competitive. It's okay to feel among sometimes. But that shouldn't be an end in itself.

Minimalists reject greed. Nothing is more against minimalist living than greed. Greed makes it easy to purchase things you do not need. It makes you insatiable, and it can make you never feel satisfied. Because it is a personality trait deeply embedded in our psyches, it is difficult to stop greed and avarice. The definition of greed is a desire to acquire everything at the cost of others, and not simply wanting more. It is a sense of contentment to see one has much, and another has very little. To overcome this trait one must be willing to share and generous. Although it can be difficult at first, it will reap its rewards. Donate any unwanted items to the Red Cross, Salvation Army, or Red Cross. You will feel lighter and more relaxed. There is nothing better than feeling like you are giving.

An emotion is just a collection of hormones your body releases into your body. It's not something you actually experience. Take control of your feelings. Don't get mad at someone who provokes you. Avoid being intimidated by a colleague's new car. Refrain from impulsive behaviors and you will discover that you make better choices all the time.

You can reduce your bad habits. All people know deep down inside their hearts that they need to get rid of bad habits. We are not able to stop ourselves from falling for these unhealthy habits. They are addictions that don't have the stigma associated with them. Smoking is bad. Excessive alcohol consumption is equally harmful. Although they may not have any noticeable negative effects, excessive TV watching or excessive sleeping can cause laziness, and low energy.

Without enjoyment, life is not worth living. You don't need to abandon your vices. The trick is to simply replace those vices with healthy ones that give you as much pleasure, if any, but are not harmful to your well-being.

It is bad to do too much, even if it is something you enjoy. If you spend more time cleaning your ears than you should, you may develop a bad habit.

I used to be very active on Twitter, but it started to affect my mental health. I became sad when I tweeted what I considered an excellent tweet, but no one retweeted. It was quite distressing to find out that someone didn't follow my back. I found it distressing that some people didn't follow me back. After a while, I suddenly thought of quitting twitter. I quit, but after about a month I returned to the site. Only after that did I realize it was a test to see how much they missed me. It seemed impossible, but I quit. I saved a lot on internet charges the first month and my phone battery began to last all day unlike before, when it needed to be charged at least twice per day. I felt less anxious than I did when I was on twitter. I also didn't want to miss out on important events. I gained way more from twitter than I lost. I was suffering from a bad addiction to twitter, but I was able to overcome it and reap the rewards.

Reduce the amount of TV that you watch, and instead use it to watch other things, like reading a book, or expanding your knowledge. You might start a new hobby that's been on your mind for a while but haven't found the time or motivation to actually do it. It's possible to do just about anything. The only thing that is certain is to replace a bad habit or decrease the time spent on one thing.

Your spending should be reduced: If you don't get rid of excess stuff you will simply go and buy new ones. The relentless, aggressive advertisements and commercials we see make us believe we have to buy things we don't. We are encouraged encourage to create a culture that values renewal and accepts things as they are. Mobile phones are purchased every year in response to a new model being released. But the truth is that the phone serves little more than its predecessor and has very little added value. This is true of operating systems as well. If Windows 7 suits your needs, you don't need Windows 8 until it becomes obsolete or too heavy.

It is a good idea ask yourself some questions before buying anything new. If I didn't have the cash to buy it right away, would I have borrowed money? Can I afford it? Is there another option that fulfills the same purpose as this one? How long is this thing likely to last? Can I get rid of it if it's not what I want? I would still buy it even if I didn't have anyone to thank me for being nice. These are questions to ask yourself before you buy anything. You will be shocked at how many times you change mind and decide to pass. This can result in more money for your wallet which is always a good thing.

Chapter 6: Effective Tips To Keep Your Home Neat And Tidy All Year

This situation is likely to happen if you are busy with many weekly tasks. You start your week with your home clean and tidy. However, by week's middle you find that your home is messy, cluttered and disorganized. It is obvious that you have not folded your dry-clean clothes properly and have left your kitchen countertop cluttered with cooking supplies and dishes. You also have clutter in your living room with toys and other household items.

Also, you find a stack of mail that has not been addressed, and clothes in your bedroom which you must address.

On Friday, you will feel like your home has been hit by a tornado. It will be hard to clean up the mess.

If you are in this frightening circle and feel like there is no escape, continue reading. These tips will transform your life as well as your home.

Tip

These effective tips will ensure that you have a relaxing weekend, free of clutter and cleaning.

Tip: Tips for organizing, cleaning, and tidying your bedroom

Storage is the most important thing to keep your bedroom tidy. The best storage solutions will ensure that your bedroom is tidy and clean.

If your bedroom doesn't have enough storage, you can buy storage containers or baskets. Storage containers that fit comfortably under your bed are the best.

The storage container can be used to store clean linen under your bed. You can also change your bed linen quickly and easily with it.

Purchase a nightstand that can be used to organize your bedroom.

Bedroom

Night time

Make sure you hang up all clothing you wore during that day.

Hang clothes items that can be worn again.

All items that have been dry cleaned should be stored in another section of your closet.

Assemble a hamper for everyone in your home.

Dust shelves and nightstands, as well as the desk

Vacuum floor and rugs.

Chapter 7: Five Signs To Make Your Life More Simple

Many people believe that an improved quality of life is the best thing. However, it is possible to realize that you should cut back on your entire life. Is your life chaotic?

Most likely, you are already intimately aware of your stressors. We often justify our worries, claim they are common and make arrangements. This article will show you how to change your perception of the world. You should take a look at these five signs to help you streamline your life.

Financial Burden

We all have at some point declined to look into our ledgers as we realized it would only add stress to us. As such, we don't want to deal with our monetary problems. You might find this a way to make a positive change that is truly necessary.

Trouble making installments? This inquiry doesn't require you to include vehicle or house payments. You may have to fight for your protection, cell bills, and utilities.

Important is the understanding that you may not have to work harder to cover these costs. Consider whether you are capable of changing the installments.

This might not seem obvious but it can be quite confusing. Lethargy and fear of managing client service delegates will often make us feel lost.

These people will not be stopped.

AT&T, a cell phone company, offers limits to employees who work for other organizations. Progressive Direct explains that there are some insurance agencies that issue lower statements for those who manage their accounts online.

You are not getting enough sleep

Because life's deterrents are present, we wake up at night thinking about what we should have done during the day and what the next day might bring. We also consider how we can expect the consequences of our actions to influence us.

The high cortisol levels in the body prevent us from getting a proper night's sleep. It makes more pressure and less time for us to awaken. As the espresso creator slowly deteriorates, he becomes the companion who facilitates each day's strain.

Even though exercise and diet do help with rest design, you can find a way to organize your life in different areas (from transportation to correspondence). Although there will be circumstances and assignments that keep us from getting too tired, it is possible to reduce the amount of stress in our lives. . Actually, I'm less concerned.

Exclusion of exploration

While you may feel that carrying out difficult tasks or data will just make your life more complicated, an absence of investigation could indicate that there is too much to be done.

We can stop looking and develop intellectually by stopping to look. Surprisingly, though, we use many reasons to not try out more things, and these reasons often highlight what is the greatest obstacle in our lives. Instead of blaming those we don't know for being troublesome, we need to manage their tightening. The guide here is that our demeanor toward new things radically influences the intricacy/effortlessness of our lives by expanding/diminishing pressure levels.

Disorganization

Disorganization is worse than losing your keys to the car or paying your bills. Not only is disorganization a sign that you may have to scale down but it also could be an indicator that you are distracted or too tired to clean.

It is important to be clear that this isn't a consolation prize. Instead, it is an update showing how neat you are. Next time your feet are covered in cups, papers and coverings, consider why they have congregated. They will look back and mock your inability or willingness to use structure and construction in your life. Leave them a lesson.

Chapter 8: The Next Steps

You can only start minimalism by clearing out your environment. [5] You can concentrate on your inner life by removing clutter from your environment and practicing taking control. We now move onto the underlying causes.

Clutter could be an indicator of emotional or psychological anguish. Is it possible that you are trying to avoid conflict or fear? Do you pretend that a relationship can be more satisfying than it is?

Although you can live like this, it is not happiness. Many people try to hide their thoughts by engaging in chatter or other activities. If you are unable to think about it, it is unlikely it is true. This is where accountability begins. This is where happiness can be found.

Begin by reviewing your daily habits to determine how healthy you are. In this context, "Healthy" means how well each habit serves your emotional, mental and spiritual needs. Health is personal because everyone has different psychological and biological factors. Although I am not going to tell you what is healthy or not; I will recommend a balanced lifestyle.

Our brains are wired to form habits and breaking them can lead to new ones. Examine the effects of your habits on your daily life. If I forget to eat breakfast, then I get hungry and eat what I find. That is a changeable behavior with a known root cause.

It is important to set small goals in order to make a change. I set a goal of eating breakfast, and I plan to achieve it by pre-making meals and keeping a few muffins on hand.

What routines could you modify in your daily life to establish good habits? Next, try it for a week. Keep a few reminder notes for cleaning up after dinner and to complete one chore per day. You could also pre-package veggies as a snack. The weekly or monthly goals will help you see more and motivate you to do more. Also, small goals increase intention and draw your attention towards new things. This can help to boost feelings of achievement.

One key to creating changes is to keep your focus on one thing at time and slowly incorporate it into your lifestyle. If a particular habit is beginning to slip, you can refocus. Some habits can be altered simultaneously. A good example is taking a morning walk. Most people believe that changing your routine takes three weeks. Make sure you stick to that time frame. Matt Cutts' TED talk is a powerful reminder to try something new for 30 consecutive days. This will give you enough time and space to either change a bad habit or drop it. It is true when he said that one month is not daunting. For a month, we can accomplish anything. It's not worth wasting time, but it is worthwhile to develop good habits.

Every action, or habit, is formed by a combination factors. What underlying forces are at work in your life today? What are the reasons for these routines? Habits can be formed through parental guidance, savvy marketing, psychological tricks or our senses. You need to brush your teeth every day, so some routines are very important. Some routines are based on societal pressures. The key to solving the problem is to identify the source.

True beginners to this process claim that things are fine. While you might not like to admit to your problems with relationships or to hate your job, clutter doesn't necessarily make it worse. Actually clutter can be a sign that there is a deeper problem. Insecurity, for example, can lead to hoarding. Because clutter visually shows value and proves you aren't in poverty, it is also a sign that you have a deeper problem. Boredom may be displayed by displaying meaningless collections or diversions. In order to get someone's attention, you might be displaying shallow relationships. Take some time to examine your relationship and identify the issues.

Although I'm not a therapist or anything, this list sums up how stuck and unhappy I felt about my life. I felt like an incompetent person and I didn't admit it for long. Though it is difficult to acknowledge feelings of inadequacy emotionally, these thoughts are detrimental to one's well-being. First, acknowledge that life is not perfect. Next, take responsibility for what you can.

[Disclaimer] Decluttering won't automatically make your life easier, or solve deeper problems. The effects of abuse or clinical anxiety are not going to disappear. But, simple exercises may be helpful in the recovery process.

Your reactions and actions are all you can control. Every decision you make has a consequence. Let's consider relationships, for instance. Is there an absence of boundaries at any point? Are needs not being met? Is technology limiting our ability to spend meaningful time together? What options are available to strengthen a relationship?

Your best life is dependent on your decisions. You can achieve happiness by being mindful and intentional. This means focusing on healthy habits and eliminating unnecessary ones.

Unexpected realities

While the promise of true happiness and fulfillment may be appealing, being your best self requires some growth pains.

Your friendships might change. What do you know about recovering alcoholics who need to avoid their bar buddies? Your priorities can cause your friendships to change. Your conversations can be affected by a social media halt or refusal to gossip. Cutting your cable means that you won't be able to participate in the conversations around 'Primetime TV programs'. Without regular updates, it can lead to friendships being put on the back burner. It is OK. After some relaxation, you can choose the role it will play in your life.

The truth is found with mindfulness. It's possible to stop focusing on your distractions (mental chatter/noise, media) and discover that you don't really like yourself. Perhaps you are having difficulties with your relationships. This realization can be devastating, but you do have the power to change. Begin to practice gratitude, generosity, responsibility.

The same goes for identity. We often define ourselves through products or job positions. A party starts with the question, "What do your job?" This is a great question because it allows you to be yourself and not your possessions.

These drawbacks are made to disappear by happiness. These drawbacks have many other benefits.

Creativity thrives. Creativity is an expression of one's self. By focusing more on yourself and removing externalities, you will find the inspiration and time needed to create.

You will feel more confident when you are done with the comparison game. You are accountable for your actions and are better able see your strengths. True confidence is being able to identify who you are and what your contribution is. It's not a crippling feeling when others make fun of you.

A decrease in anxiety. Removing yourself from the toxic people and bustle will be a huge help. Plus, a clear space will bring more clarity. Even if toxic people are your only option, it can be healing to find some peace within.

It's possible to save money. Many people realize minimalism as a side effect of a fast spending lifestyle. By avoiding unnecessary expenses, you can build any kind of savings account and pay off your debt quickly. By meal planning, for example, you can plan your shopping list and know exactly what you'll be buying. By sticking to your grocery lists and avoiding late-night eating out, you can save money. This will allow you to keep your money, as you won't be tempted to buy clearance items.

Give up minimalism

Minimalism can be used as a tool to discover your true self, and to live the life you want. But we don't have the obligation to define ourself with this term. If minimalist thoughts have served their purpose well and you're ready for change, then you can set the tool down.

Moving in a new direction does not mean you are abandoning the tool. You are exploring--intentionally--which is what this is all about.

Chapter 9: Preventing Future Clutter

The steps you have taken in the previous chapter will make a difference in the space in your house and office. You'll want to maintain order after your initial decluttering. This chapter will help you to take preventative measures to prevent clutter from returning.

1.) Incorporate cleaning up or decluttering into your daily schedule. This is especially important if you want to keep your living and work space orderly. Choose a convenient time to sort mail, organize a shelf, and straighten the closet.

Make it easy to adjust according to your daily tasks. This will help you become more habitual. As an example, if you're a mom first time, you can take fifteen to twenty minutes to declutter while your baby or toddler sleeps. Morning people can get rid of the clutter on their way out, and those who are rushing to go to work can finish it once they get back.

It is crucial that you create a schedule that works best for you, and that it is followed closely. It may seem simple, but if this step is done regularly, it can have significant results over time. This is a sure-fire way to reduce clutter.

2.) You can be creative with teaching children how clean up after them, so they start to do it at an early age. It's possible to incorporate little games in your cleaning routine. For example, you could have a race where children must put toys or books in their correct storages. Or, they can place dirty clothes into laundry hampers. It is less likely that their stuff will accumulate into overwhelming piles of clutter if your children are involved in the cleaning process.

3.) Follow the In and Out rule. The In-and-Out rule states that any item performing the same function as your new addition to the home or office will be thrown out or donated.

If you're purchasing new clothes, it is a good idea to donate or recycle the appropriate amount. This is especially important when purchasing new socks or clothing because these items last the longest.

4.) It is best to wait at least 48 hours before making impulse purchases. Don't succumb to the temptation to purchase something you don't need or want. Give yourself time. It is common for impulse buys to fade over time. This will save you both money as well as storage space.

5.) Build a special fund for travel and experience to reward yourself. This account should be used to save any money that you have saved after you've fought the urge to impulse buy. It's also helpful to assign a purpose to your account, such a future trip to an amusement park, or another destination you know you will enjoy. These experiences take up no space in your home but your mind and heart. You'll be able to resist the urge of buying next time because you know you are helping to make a greater impact.

Chapter 10: Junk The Junk Warmer

It is not worth wasting time arguing about this challenge. Let's just take it one step at a time and tackle those junk drawers. Clutter is a natural shopper and loves to be found in these junk drawers. There are a few junk drawers in my home. One by the door of the entrance, two for each person, and another at the desk in my living room. Another one is in the kitchen. Then there's the upstairs junk drawer.

Today's challenge - Reduce your junk drawers by 50% – 75%

I know this, I know it, these drawers are filled with "important stuff that is necessary". These drawers have the simplest task because they're full of small bits and pieces. We will ease into this by doing a test run or transition where we can remove some things from the drawers before actually throwing them out.

The Steps

The following can be done for every junk drawer

Step 1: Identify your target drawers. Take a close look at the list and add one or more junk areas.

Step 2: Empty out all of the areas or drawers that you are targeting.

Step 3: Separate your items into three piles.

Step 4 - Put the things you use back in the drawer. Throw out the second pile.

Step 5 - Take a critical look at everything you have. Are you keeping duplicates? Did you save something because you thought you might need it in the future? You should keep asking yourself: "What is the absolute worst thing that can happen if it gets thrown away?"

Step 6 - Find a box or a gym bag, and place the third stack in there. This is the "On Notice Bag" or transition pile. This pile will not be thrown away (yet), so please don't fret about stuffing too many items in there.

Step 7 - Take the bag you just bought and stuff it in a drawer. We are going to try it out for a couple of weeks and see if it really is necessary.

The Results

This is something I have done before (did you think I would give this untested task?) However, there was more junk in my house than I thought. If not dealt with, clutter can quickly spread like a virus. Most of the stuff that is obvious can be thrown away. Some stuff can be a challenge. Strangely, I felt a rush to get rid of some items even though they were certain "keeps" when it was the same exercise a few months before. I gave away an expensive watch that was given to me as a gift years ago but never used. It is gratifying to know that someone else will enjoy it and that it isn't taking up space within my drawer.

Additional tip: You'll find certain themes in your junk folder when you start to declutter. You can gather these items and then group them together. I keep a list of receipts in my filing cupboard. I don't organize them alphabetically but it makes it easy to locate what I need. I also keep a sandwich bag containing headphones and another bag containing all of my house keys.

YOU WILL NEED A FILING CUBINET

A filing cabinet can be one of the most useful tools for clearing clutter. I'm sure that you found yourself with a huge stack of papers when you finished yesterday's task. Get one right away if you don't have one. If you already have one, it is important to start using it properly.

Today's challenge: Use your filing cabinet effectively.

The filing cabinet doesn't have to be huge like the one in an office. It could be as small as two drawers, or even a simple accordion file with multiple pockets. A filing cabinet is a cost-effective way to prevent your important documents becoming clutter. It also helps you organize your house so that you don't have to search the entire house for one important document.

WARNING!!! It is important to not treat your filing cabinet like a trash can.).

The Steps

Step 1 - If you don't own a filing cupboard, buy one. You can purchase them online quite cheaply. Make sure you only have one or two drawers. Two drawers will provide enough space to store all your important documents. A large accordion file or several small ones can save space while being very cost-effective.

Step 2 Create your base folders. Here's an example of how you might organise things.

- Health: medical information, test results, vaccination records and doctor bills for submitting insurance applications

- Credit Card & Bank Account Statements: These folders can be used if necessary. However, I recommend that you choose to receive your statements online (discussed later).

- Historic taxes: Each tax year should have a separate folder. It's best to keep your taxes up to seven years, if you really want to get technical.

- Upcoming Taxes - Make sure you are calm on April 15th. Get organized by gathering the documents that you will need to file your current tax year, such as W-2s, donation receipts and copies of moving expenses.

- Home: Information related to your current house, like your lease or mortgage documents

- Instruction manuals: This category is for all instructions manuals that you may require in the future. Some of these manuals are online, but many others can be downloaded from the internet.

- Receipts. Keep all receipts that may be needed later in here. Did you purchase a TV? Or another expensive item that you wanted to test out before you bought it? Be sure to keep receipts but not too many.

- Car: Purchase record, title, warranty, insurance

- Sentimental is a collection for sentimental papers like certificates and diplomas.

Step 3 - Go through your paper stacks and sort them into the files that you have made. If you find papers that do not fit in one of these categories, create additional folders. You don't need hundreds upon hundreds of folders. A "general" folder will save you time and help you to organize your papers.

Step 4: While you're going, be aware that you are also trying decrease your paper clutter. You should always ask yourself "Can I throw this away" and "What happens if I don't use it later?" If you don't have a substantial trash pile at the finish, then you are not doing this right.

* * * *

The Results

I have organized my papers before into my filing cabinet. But it's always worth going back and making more space. This task made me realize that I should make more use of my filing cabinet. So I started to gather my papers around my house and spent approximately 20 minutes putting it away. I have a habit of organizing my folders so I was able quickly to file the new papers.

Additional tip: You will almost certainly have a lot of papers that you need to throw out once you are done. These papers will likely contain a lot personal information so choose where to put them. It is best to shred these papers and put them in a secure place where potential identity thieves cannot access them.

Chapter 11: Start Early

So that you don't have to wait for your "eager friends" and family to interfere with your decision-making, it is best to begin as early as possible. You can always start to clean out basements and closets if you need to sell your home before moving.

Keep in mind that packing too many items at once will lead to you searching for things for months.

To make sure you don't waste their time and effort, be prepared to assign a few tasks to your outside helpers. The kitchen is an area where outside helpers can work. You need the kitchen most up-to-the day of the move. These items will also be the first to be unpacked and used when you move in. This applies to the bathroom as well.

CARRY A NOTICEBOOK

You should always have a small spiral notepad with you. It will fit in your pocket or purse, so it can be quickly accessed. You can use it to write down a solution while you wait for a prescription or dinner partner. You will use this notebook as your guide. Retractable tape measure is also a good option.

LABEL LABEL LABEL

It is undoubtedly the most important thing you can do! Label the containers and boxes that you are packing. It saves time and effort when you need to find something after the move. Inside labels can direct you to the quarry. You can write the contents of the box on a sheet or paper with a magic pencil and then tape it to the box.

COLOR CODE

Unpacking will be easier if you use color code. Use different colors in different rooms. For example, blue labels for basement storage boxes; red for the kitchen; green for the master bedrooms. Moving companies can place color-coded boxes into the appropriate rooms, making it easier for you to pack. This is a great idea! It has worked great during two office moves.

CONTAINERS

Use empty copies paper boxes to store your items. These wonderful items may not be available to you, but office supply stores carry great cardboard and plastic storage boxes in many sizes. I used wallpaper to cover the boxes containing items that I knew I would keep for a long period of time. I covered one box with a map of my home to cover it, while some blueprints were used to cover another box that held papers from my old houses.

ORGANIZE RECORDS

You should keep all records in separate file files (again from an Office Supply Store) and clearly mark them so that you can easily retrieve them when you are looking for them. Do not put similar items in the same file folder. Put together, for example, insurance policies; Social Security documents; financial statements; and your Will and Trust paper.

LEAVE A PAPER TRAIL

It is a great opportunity to leave a "paper trace" for your family in case of your death or disability. A CURRENT list should be prepared of all assets, including your retirement plans and insurance policies. You should tell your family where to find this "paper trails", as well as your Will. A fireproof box or safe deposit box can be kept at home. The safety deposit box or security box should be accessible to a family member.

BOOKS

My most difficult possession was books. You must be brutal when it comes to moving. Ask yourself this question: "Will it ever happen again?" If the answer to that question is "No", then give the books or sell them to a used bookstore. BEGINNING EARLY WITH THIS PROJECT IS IMPORTANT.

FRAMED PHOTOS

How about all those framed family photographs? All but the most important photos should be removed from their frames. Use the album to be a coffee table or desk book. Enjoy the photos!

LOOSE Snapsticks

There are several options to solve the problem of a large number of unorganized snapshots in a household. If you have time and the desire to organize them, give each of your kids a selection of photos from the extended family, such as aunts, uncles or cousins. This will allow them to start their own collection.

If you are not yet ready to share your pictures and they have not been put into albums, you can place them, along with any newer ones, in a pretty basket. Keep the basket handy so others can browse them and enjoy them as much as you. You should date the photos and identify their subjects.

FURNITURE TO REMOVE

We're getting serious. These suggestions are for items that you will not be able to take to your new place. Offer to give the items you hate to parting with to your family. If they accept, then you will be able to "visit" your children. You have two options: sell the rest, or give them to charity. The receipts of the charity should be kept for income tax preparation next year. Avoid making the mistake of older people who keep too many pieces of furniture. They end up with cramped spaces that look like a furniture store.

FURNITURE YOU WANT TO KEEP

It's much more difficult to decide what you will do with the rest. Drawing a floor plan for your home with a friend is a good idea. You can then "place", your furniture using pieces you've cut out to the right scale. This will help you to know exactly what won't go.

QUESTION MAKING PIECES

If you're still uncertain about one or more of your pieces, bring these "question marks", and you can decide when you get to the new house. DON'T TAKE ANYTHING AWAY UNTIL IT IS CERTAIN YOU CAN NOT USE IT!

Chapter 12: Simplify Your Life With Contentment

Finding happiness is difficult when you have to deal with daily grinds and modern society's desire for more. Working and going to school can often make us feel stuck and disconnected from the things we love. There's no reason for us to be satisfied with this.

You should not confuse contentment with giving up or settling for less. It is a state where you are satisfied with yourself, aware of your capabilities, and confident that you can live in freedom from society's pressures, and work steadily towards what you desire. Do you think this sounds like a worthy pursuit of your goals?

Knowing how to improve your confidence can make it easier to live in happiness. To simplify your life and live a happy life, use the following tips.

Be kind to yourself and others

However, this should not be taken literally in every situation. Sometimes it is helpful to compare yourself to others in order to gain inspiration or recognize when you have made mistakes.

This suggestion is specifically meant to stop you doing two things. First, compare yourself to people at different points in your life. Second, conform to popular tastes. Let's go over each one.

How can you compare yourself with people at a different level of life? It is an unjust comparison that will place you at a grave disadvantage.

We sometimes fail to consider the needs, goals and ambitions of others, and our successes in these areas can make us feel a little less successful. However, life isn't a race. This attitude can cause you to be unable to accept the challenges of life and force you to sacrifice your desires in return for the goods of another.

Also, conforming to popular opinions can cause you to lose your sense of fulfillment, which is a major component to contentment. Instead of focusing your attention on and exploring your passions, you become uninterested in the world around you. As if all this wasn't enough, think about how unhappy it can make you feel to realize that you've allowed society to mold you.

Live in Moderation

Follow the Middle Way in Buddhist terms. To put it another way, try to find a balance between self indulgence and giving up what brings you joy. Both are equally destructive, and both leave us wanting more.

Do you find yourself a self-indulgent person? Consider how moderation can simplify life.

Experiment has shown us that being satisfied with what we want doesn't satisfy our needs. It actually spoils us. It is possible to limit the amount of food, media, and other items you consume. You eventually will be content with less and can focus on other things instead of having more.

If you are unable to enjoy your pleasures, you'll be very unhappy. Your life will likely be complicated by your insatiable cravings, envy, or internal conflict. Be mindful that too much self-discipline could make it difficult to be stern about the things that truly make life worthwhile.

Be surrounded by what you love

Surrounding yourself with your most treasured things is the best way to find happiness. Being surrounded by people, things and objects we love gives us the ability to release our anxieties and remind ourselves of our strengths. You must not underestimate the effects of your environment.

Create a space that is welcoming and nurturing. This should be a lot of fun and will produce a completely different result for everyone. Roger Dean and Martin Dean are just two examples. One brother loves to create in inspiring surroundings, while the other prefers quieter spaces. Discover what inspires you to enjoy your favourites often.

Shun Complacency

Being content means being in a place that isn't boring and that allows you to look forward to stimulating new ideas. Complacency is not a good synonym for contentment. This can cause us to lose our ability to improve and be self-congratulatory.

This is not a state you should be living in if your goal is to be truly fulfilled. This suggestion is to stop focusing on your job or home. It is important to continually question your beliefs, morals, and practices. This great way of growing can be done anywhere, in privacy.

Take Your Time

You are concerned about meeting deadlines, and following a schedule. You may even feel that this suggestion is wishful thinking. Surprisingly, it only takes a little bit more courage and initiative to take your time. Once you start to do this, you will see that it can make you happier. You can start by taking your time and ensuring you do a great job in every activity.

This is a good thing for your work life. It means you are less likely to be criticized by your boss and more revisions on your own. Even if your passion is to be busy, taking time off will help you take stock and appreciate your contributions. You can improve the flow of your day by slowing things down and seeing the results.

Chapter 13: Make Gratitude A Discipline

A minimalist lifestyle requires gratitude.

If you are grateful, you will be content and more thankful for the many blessings in your life. A grateful heart will make you more optimistic, which can increase your enthusiasm and drive to fulfill your passions. You will experience a healthy sense of mindfulness when you are grateful. It will be easier for you to slow down and appreciate your blessings. A grateful heart will make it easier to give your attention to other people. When you get involved in the lives of others, your life will be more fulfilling. If you are grateful, you will find it easier and more enjoyable to help others. Being humble enough to recognize that other people's help can also bring you joy will make it easier for you to be grateful. A grateful heart will help you attract good friends and generous people into you life.

Research shows gratitude is linked to a higher mental awareness and a healthier physique. You'll feel happier and more appreciative for the good things in your life. Not only will it give you strength to conquer the difficulties and hurdles you will surely face, but it will also help you be grateful for the good times.

Grit can be finicky, it is true. You'll find that it is much easier to be grateful during certain moments in your life. If everything is going smoothly in your world, such as a happy family, a home that is warm and comfortable, a good job, and your children doing well at school, it can be quite easy to be grateful.

It can be hard to find something to be grateful when you are going through difficult times. Sometimes it can be hard to feel grateful even when you are facing difficult times in your own life. When everything is going wrong, it may be hard to be grateful. It is important to remember that the darkest times are those when you need to be grateful. Those are the times where gratitude can provide you with the strength, perspective, and optimism you need to get through all the difficulties.

The time you most need gratitude is the one when it seems the most distant. We have come to believe that gratitude can be a response to our current situations. Reacting with gratitude is an easy thing to do when things are going well. It can be very difficult to express thankfulness during difficult times.

No matter your circumstances, gratitude will help you feel more grateful. The discipline of gratitude requires consistent practice and attention, just as with other disciplines. You should practice it when life is going well but even more, when it's not. You'll eventually learn to be grateful if you practice gratitude consistently.

Chapter 14: Accept The Fact That You Will Always Need Bills To Pay

Visualize your monthly bills.

Take into account your grocery receipts, gas and electric bill and cell phone bills. Add to that the cost you have to pay for recent medical office copays, tests, xrays, and lab work. Add to that your monthly water and trash bills, as well as your auto insurance. All due in the following days.

Now, imagine your checkbook.

Every bill you pay online and by hand comes out of your checking account. Look at the numbers, as you probably have many times in the past.

If you're like most people you feel the same way when you examine your expenses. We spent three more trips to the supermarket because we had to cater to out-oftown guests last weekend. There's also the receipt from Thursday's dinner out, the gasoline receipt, and the recharge for the Starbucks card. Wait! Amazon has a receipt - actually, two receipts. One was for the leaf-blower replacement and the other for the graduation present that we bought for our niece.

Keep an eye on the balance while you pay bills and account for them. If you don't have enough money to pay your bills, your balance will decrease. Sometimes, it can be heart-wrenching to see this happen. It can cause anxiety, stress, and a sense loss. It can even cause resentment, depending upon the nature of the bills.

The solution to such feelings can be found in your working years. You can rely on the recurring income you receive from your paycheck to replenish and renew the funds you eventually spend. Your paycheck can be your wellspring. It is your fuel. It is your source for energy and continued sustenance.

It is an ever-present struggle between what income you earn and what you spend. You can budget in various ways to keep your head above water. This could take the form of careful planning, or the practice of moderation. Sometimes, guilt can be a motivator to stay on track. Sometimes, panic can set in.

Now, imagine that you have reached retirement age.

All of these spending examples mentioned above could happen in your 80s as well as in your 30s, 40s, and 50s. Each of these costs is common and recurring. It is possible to purchase a home or cars and other luxury items but you will still need to make basic living expenses.

No matter what age you are, your basic needs will not disappear.

Let's just say that, regardless of age, basic expenses will never disappear.

The difference is that you, as a retiree may have very little to no steady income available to replenish your account balances. This raises a fundamental question: How will you, your spouse, generate a steady stream of income to pay your ongoing expenses when you retire.

You can't simply divide what you've saved by your expected life expectancy. Because no one knows when they'll live, this is why it's so difficult to calculate. What if your life expectancy is significantly higher? Many think that they can increase their sustainability by keeping the money that they don't spend and investing it in anticipation for "historical average" returns. But what if markets crash and you have less money to make income?

In younger years, your paycheck replenished you and replaced any money you were forced to spend. Is there any way to ensure the same thing happens when you retire. Is there a way to get an "income forever" that doesn't depend on the market? It will pay no matter what you do.

The upcoming rules will address these questions.

As of now, it is essential to understand and not forget that your bills will be there throughout retirement. This is real cash that must be used and will soon be lost forever. It can't be saved, reinvested, nor left to heirs.

Financial security in retirement can only be achieved if you have the ability to consistently pay your bills no matter how long you live. This is true for you, for your spouse, for your parents, and any other person who wants financial safety and security in retirement.

Spend less than you make

In the first rule we mentioned that certain bills will always stay with us regardless of how long our lives. It is vital to take the time to contemplate what your ongoing expenses will be when you retire. It is important to consider your expected retirement expenses and your sources of retirement income.

Your income must be higher than your expenses. And especially in this era of multidecade retirements, spending more than your income is like sailing in a boat full holes.

No, wait. It's worse.

This is because you are not in the boat. The "you" you think of today is most likely your current, strong, invincible, ready-to-face-future-challenges self. The boat is where you will find your future self. Your old-age self. You may have an old-age spouse with you. This is an extremely fragile time. It's also the worst time of your boat's life to burst or capsize.

Although it is easy to grasp the virtues of spending less than your income, it is not as simple to live a life that is financially sustainable. You will be advised to gather your strength and set a budget in most financial books. For many, strict budgeting works well for some but is not for everyone. Human nature is such that people will resist any budget restrictions. Too much sacrifice. Too much discipline. Too much willpower. It's too hard to stick with the plan for the long-term.

This fact is made more difficult by the unpredictable nature future expenses. You will be surprised at the unexpected expenses that life can throw at you, as any household manager knows. These unexpected expenses are very difficult to predict and can cause budgets to become shaky.

I would like you to consider an alternative to strict spending. This is the solution I'll be using to solve various problems posed by these rules. Instead of focusing solely on establishing a strict budget, instead focus on establishing strict routines. Some examples:

Grandma used Christmas gifts to spend too much on her grandchildren. How? How did she do it? Her expenses never rise, even if she gets more grandkids. She doesn't spend too much because she has a regular routine. She knows how much money she will require ahead of time. The grandchildren enjoy it too, and they look forward to spending "Grandma's money."

Alicia loves to eat out with Tom, but they realized that they were spending way too much on it each month. Instead of spending Friday evenings at a fancy restaurant, they decided to go to their favorite place for breakfast every Friday morning. They shared a big breakfast menu item. They enjoy each other's company and the good food. It is often a fraction than what they would have spent otherwise. Their "date morning in" is something they look for each week and is consistent with their long-term goal of not spending too much.

Jane and Allen were discussing the fact that, although they loved traveling to other places for weekend getaways, it was quite costly. They discovered that they did not spend much time looking for fun activities to do close by home. They began to search for local attractions. The community bike path was something that stood out. In the evenings they began to take short walks along this trail for exercise. The trail, which was once part of a railroad line, cuts through some stunning scenic woods. The couple bought bikes and soon began to ride the trail as often as five times per week. These outings allow them to keep fit, give them quality time, and provide hours worth of enjoyment for virtually no cost.

With examples like these, I could go on forever. They are an example of a very important secret that many people struggle with understanding. The secret to spending less is not about sacrifice or willpower, but about creating routines that are well-planned and aligned. Willpower does have a role, but it is not what drives the engines. We will also be talking about other topics such as nutrition, exercise, health, how to make your family happy, investing success, and how to better manage your time.

As formulas:

Failure is the combination of the best budget and the same old routine.

Success is possible with a new, better routine and more time!

What are your priorities, and how do they influence your daily life?

If you are looking for optimal body weight but have a passion for baking sugary cookies and watching cooking shows, Do you want less alcohol but to spend weekends with friends who seem to always end up at a bourbon and cigar bar on weekends? You would like to learn more about your profession while binge-watching crime series on the weekends.

If this is the case, your routines, or regular actions, are not in line with your long term goals. Without making a lifestyle change, it will be difficult to achieve what you want.

It is important to have a daily lifestyle that is consistent with your desire to spend less. The prime movers of success are not "limits"," "deprivation", "willpower," nor "willpower."

Success is achieved through words such as: "deliberate", 'intentional," "designed," and "aligned."

Spend some time listing the things that you spend money on. It is possible to feel resentful about the item or that they are costing more than you want. You should list all ongoing monthly expenses over $300 per calendar month.

In a 25-30 years retirement, $300 per month will equal approximately $100,000. Do regular expenses come in at $600 each month? That's $200,000.

Decide whether the expenses are worth the investment. Consider lifestyle changes that reflect your values and help you to eliminate or reduce these ongoing expenses.

Chapter 15: Emotionally Dealing A Minimalist Life Style

Personal emotion is the single biggest obstacle to living a minimalist life.

Many people don't realize that they are emotionally connected with their belongings until it's too late. This connection can take many forms, most often in the form guilt. No matter what age they are, adults often feel guilty if they need to get rid.

Don't you think it's a shame to throw away the towel set that Auntie bought you?

Isn't it rude not to give away the crock pot that you received for your wedding?

Do you not think it would be rude to throw away the quilt you've owned for 10+ years, but your grandmother bought it?

A minimalist lifestyle is one that allows you to live in a clutter-free home and let go of any annoyances, anger, guilt or sadness.

The four main reasons why people keep items is to:

1) The item retains sentimental value

2) The item might prove useful one day

3) The item costs a lot

4) The item was purchased as a present

These items will be discussed so that you can begin thinking about how your emotions may impact your ability (or inability!) to get rid clutter. Don't forget that minimalism doesn't necessarily mean you need to throw away all your favourite things. You don't have to sell your CD collection or give your child's first outfit away. The only thing you need is to stop buying the third crockpot or the books you haven't read in years.

1) The item retains sentimental value

It's not just that the ratty old tee shirt you have on your shelf is two sizes too small.

You won't find a piece of fabric that has been stained in 10 years.

You don't need to wear the same old clothes.

What you see are the clothes you wore when your husband first proposed to you. You see the Ferris Wheel. You see popcorn. You see silly games, laughter, crowds, and laughter.

On the outside it is just a shirt.

To you, it's much more.

Every day, hundreds of different things come into our lives. We have toys, books, computers and clothes. These things are what make us happy and help us connect with the people around our world.

But it isn't the objects that make our lives extraordinary.

It's people and their experiences.

Decluttering your home will bring back both good and bad memories. As you go through each item in your closet, or on the bottom of your drawers, you'll be able to see what you have. It is important to accept our pasts when you are downsizing. You have to decide if the things you are holding on to, whether it is your ex-girlfriends' favorite DVD or receipts from the days you had fun.

Take a look at the item and ask yourself these questions:

Do I really want this?

How can I use it?

Do I like it?

Why am I keeping this?

You can get rid of anything in your life. It's okay not to stop moving forward with your lives. It is OK to move on in your life. It is okay to dispose of items you no longer use or need. You aren't denying the memories, experiences, or people you have shared this item with.

Sometimes you have to let go to move on.

This is fine.

2) The item might prove useful someday

Potentially Useful Disorder is where you are saving things like twine, ribbon or clothes that don't suit you.

Sometimes, people just keep an item "just incase."

Sometimes, it's a wise decision to hold onto items. It's a smart idea to hold onto things if you intend to have another one. This is good common sense. It is not wise to keep things you don't use or bought that you forgot about.

It can be hard to get rid off things you may not use. If you do, it is essentially admitting that the hobby failed or that you didn't achieve your goals. Let's take, for instance, that you wanted to learn how crochet. So you bought a lot of yarn, crochet hooks, and other tools. The end result was that you didn't like it and now you have a lot of crochet stuff.

However, you may want to keep it for another day. It's okay to stop now.

You do know what?

That's fine.

It is okay not to like or enjoy something. There is nothing wrong with not being able to enjoy something. While you may enjoy something, it's not wrong to be too busy to do it right now.

Get rid off the junk.

If you choose to return to the hobby, it is possible to buy something similar.

3) The item costs a lot

The cost of new products is high.

Even designer pieces on sale may be quite expensive.

It can be very difficult to part ways with an item you have paid a lot of money for. It's possible that you have at least a few items you still love because you paid a lot of money for them.

Stop!

Ask yourself, "Is that really worth it?"

If you don't use something, it's best to get rid of it. It doesn't matter how much you spent or what it cost. If you aren't using it, it isn't meeting your needs. It should be thrown out.

4) The item was purchased as a present

Aunt Polly likely had your best interest in mind when she bought you this leather jacket. Even though you are vegan and don't like it, it is impossible to let go of the jacket.

Why?

Because it was a gift.

It was also a gift from someone that you love.

We all have them: the unwelcome gifts.

We all have things on our shelves that are hard to part with.

This is a recipe to clutter your life. Give it to someone you love. They gave it to you in hopes that you would use and love it. After you have finished using the gift, you can throw it away and get on with your life. Gifts don't have to stay put.

Tip: Consider keeping a gift for six month if you are given it. It is okay to give it away, even if you don't make use of it for that amount of time.

Chapter 16: Do The Math

*Complete these worksheets using your spiral notebook to calculate your downsizing.

*You will need a calculator.

WORKSHEET A: COMPARE CURRENT & NEW SQUARE FOOTAGE

Note: If the square footage is not known or important, you can skip this worksheet.

Calculate the percentage loss in square feet

4. Divide the difference in line 3 by the square footage at current (line 1 above), to get a percentage. Round the percentage to the nearest whole percent if necessary.

*This percentage shows the amount of possess space to have an identical level of fullness to your

*This is your minimum reduction goal.

*Example - If your current square footage measures footage will be 1200 sq. 800 sq. ft. is how much sc move. By dividing 800 by 2, you will get 40%. Your r the size of your old one. This would require that you (possessions.

WORKSHEETB : COMPARE CURRENT TO A
NEW NUMBER OF LIVING SPACES ROOMS

(DO NOT include basement, attic, garage, sheds, etc.)

Notice: Please include (or remove) bathrooms from include bathrooms from #2.

1. Keep track of the rooms that you are using.

2. Make a list of the rooms that you would like to hav

3. Add 2 to 1 to get the difference. This is the differ line 3. Line 3: The difference is how many rooms you'

Calculate the percentage lost rooms:

4. Divide the difference (line 3) by the current ro
percentage you'll be losing in living-space. This p
5. Round the percentage up to the nearest whole

*This percentage shows how many possessions y
space that is similar to the one you have.

*This is Your Goal for Downsizing.

*Example. Let's say that your current number is 10, and you add six more rooms. Line 3 shows the difference. Divide 6 by 10 to find out that there will be 60% less room in your new home. About 60% of your possessions will need to be downsized.

Calculate what percentage of your kitchen cabinets will be lost:

4. Divide the difference (line three above) with the current number cabinets (line one above).

You can use line 4 to calculate a percentage. Round the percentage to obtain the nearest whole percentage if necessary.

You will need to reduce the kitchen cabinet space by dividing 5 by 15. To reduce your kitchen's size by 33%, you will need to downsize some items.

*Note - This doesn't take into account the dimensions of each cabinet but gives an approximate estimate of what percentage you can reduce.

WORKSHEET D: ROOM ANALYSIS

At the top page of your notebook, write down every room you'll lose. Each room should be noted:

Large pieces you won't be able take with you

Take large pieces of jewelry with you

--Items you need for sorting (pieces you won't take, built in shelving, boxes etc.)

These rooms make a great place to start your decluttering.

Chapter 17: Minimalism in relation to Consumerism

You can do more with less. --Robert Browning, 1855 poem Andrea del Sarto

Minimalism isn't about a lack or a dearth of something. It's just the right amount. --Nicholas Burroughs (graphic designer)

In recent years, minimalism has gained popularity online and offline. What is minimalism, exactly? Why is minimalism so popular? What is the benefit of being a minimalist person?

Minimalism leaves space for the essentials.

Some people might have preconceived notions of minimalism. Minimalism may be associated with sacrifice and deprivation. If they think of minimalism, they might think of Zen, Austerity, Zen, and other religious and spiritual movements. Maybe they think of minimalist architecture and art. Some people find minimalism boring and uninteresting, which leads them to embrace maximalism.

There are also those who think minimalism is too strict and say people should be more careful about living simple lives.

These are extreme views on minimalism. They are not completely incorrect or unfounded. But they give an incomplete view of minimalism.

Minimalism is an approach to living that encourages a deeper understanding of one's own life and helps you identify and eliminate the unnecessary. Minimalism refers to moderation and simple life. It is finding harmony, with the heart the fulcrum.

Let's make some analogies in order to better understand the concept. Minimalism is not indulgence, nor yo yo dieting. It is living a balanced, healthy lifestyle. Financial minimalism, if we take finance as a metaphor, is neither squandering, nor stinginess. But it is allocating money wisely. When we compare childrearing to minimalism, it isn't about neglecting or patronizing your children but rather allowing them to flourish in the real world.

These examples demonstrate that minimalism is a balance act. It doesn't place importance on loss but on gain. The positive is more important than the negative. It isn't restriction, it's freedom. Freedom from materialism. Freedom to focus on people, relationships, happiness and abundance and following one's passions.

The metaphors also illustrate how minimalism can transcend all aspects. Although a minimalist lifestyle may be started with the goal of decluttering their physical space, it can also spread to other areas of one's life such as finances, health, and family.

Once you commit your heart to minimalism it seems that it will come into your life. It can change your life and you'll find yourself applying its principles every day.

Here's a recap of the original definition of minimalism. Minimalalism is not about ignoring the myths surrounding it. It is about focusing on what really matters and getting back to the essence. It is more than merely allowing space to be freed up. It is about making space to store the essentials. This journey is not about stopping at the destination. Minimalism is the journey and not the destination. Perhaps you'll find the positive effects of minimalism radiating throughout your life.

Minimalism isn't something you just do. You have to make it happen. You have to be passionate about it. You have to choose minimalism. This brings us to minimalism's second definition. It is a way of life and a mindset.

Minimalism promotes personal responsibility.

Laurie Buchanan, Purposeful Living Advocate, stated that minimalism is about making space for living simply and meaningfully. It's all about living intentionally.

Minimalism is a personal choice. It is a personal choice that requires reflection. This leads to an intention and action that creates a path that is unique for each individual.

It's easy to lose sight on this uniqueness because minimalism has become so mainstream. People often only see the result.

Some people believe minimalism is simply a numbers game.

Carla is a minimalist and has 100 things in her Zen-like apartment. Mike wins the race because he has 60 of his own items and lives in an apartment. Sandra lives in a studio unit and owns 40 items. Rick has 20 items, which he carries with him as he travels all over the globe. But wait! Monk Ling is the best because it doesn't matter what he owns.

Colin Wright and other minimalist gurus are starting to move away from listing the items they own in an effort to change the perception that minimalist living is all a matter of owning few things or being thrifty.

Minimalism doesn't mean you have to adopt a certain lifestyle. It is up to you to find out what works and not.

A stereotype states that minimalists are typically males wearing black clothing. You might think of people like Steve Jobs, Mark Zuckerberg, Barack Obama, etc. who wear the exact same outfit every day. Maybe you are familiar with minimalist authorities Colin Wright Joshua Fields Millburn , Ryan Nicodemus. You may be able to form a stereotype about a minimalist personality by reading about them. The truth is that minimalism comes in many forms.

Minimalism involves more than just the external effort (practices like reducing personal possessions and simplifying your wardrobe), and the external outcome. This refers to the results or manifestations (clutter-free space, signature clothing style). Minimalism starts in the internal process of choice and consciousness. This inevitably leads to actions, and ultimately results.

External effort and result without internal processing touch the superficial only. Although minimalism can be a quick fix for people who want to get rid of unnecessary stuff, it is possible that they will revert to their old consumerist ways if there is not a fundamental change in their thinking, heart and beliefs.

On the flip side, one might experience material austerity, spiritual asceticism or other internal processes. However, it's not fair to compare minimalism to such results. It is possible to have 10 kids, a large house, and still practice minimalism. A shoe collector might find joy in the pursuit of 1000+ shoes and still be able to practice minimalism. It is possible to continue your passion for trying different cuisines while still practicing minimalism. It is possible to keep a unique and colorful wardrobe and still follow minimalism. It is possible to choose to remain employed rather than start a business and still follow minimalism.

Minimalism is a personal and individual journey. What you consider not-essential in your daily life might be essential for someone else. That's the beauty and joy of it all. When you let go all of your nonessentials, let yourself also let go any judgements of what the other person considers essential.

Another analogy to this internal process is minimalism. It's a way of awakening the self. Marketing and advertising have conditioned us to consumerism from a young age. Perhaps it is because of our social and cultural influences, such as school, work, friends, and family, that we are conditioned to believe in conspicuous consumption, indulgence, extravagance, or other consumeristic behaviors.

It is possible that we have lost touch our inner voice amid all the noise. We reach that tipping moment when we become tired of the consumer noise and start hearing a whisper deep within that tells us we might need a review of our priorities.

Minimalism can be seen in terms of a spectrum.

You can look deep within yourself and ask: Where do I want to go? Where are I going? What are my plans to get there This topic will be explored in the following chapters.

Let us dive deeper into our exploration of minimalism. We will be referring to just right minimalism throughout this book.

Some people are negative about minimalism, and they avoid living this lifestyle. They believe it's too dangerous. Some people believe you have to get rid of everything material in order to be minimalist. But is that really true? What is minimalism relative to consumerism and what does it mean? What is minimalism and how does it relate to austerity

Minimalism neutralizes consumerism.

Let us now examine the etymology. Minimalism is Latin for minimus which means smallest. Consumption comes from the Latin term consumere, which is a combination de con meaning with or thoroughly and sumere indicating take or buy.

Minimalism places emphasis on the simplest, most essential things. Consumerism is focused on collective consumption. This is in line with the view of consumerism's macro benefits. It can help push the economy forward but it can also be problematic when consumers turn it to an incessant and unexamined accumulation material possessions. An obsession to satisfy external or global cravings that blocks the realization of inner desires.

The obsession with external happiness can lead to excessive spending, debt, and clutter. This will negate the quality of one's life and make it less enjoyable. It is possible to be fortunate or hardworking and end up wealthy and successful. However, without inner change, the same person may feel empty inside or be unsatisfied.

The following table summarises differences between consumerism, minimalism, and other forms of minimalism.

Consumerism	Minimalism
Needs	Not enough
Excess	Enough
Superfluous	Necessary
Consume	Incorporate
Profligate	Productive
Self-Indulgence	Contribution
Breadth	Depth
Accumulation	Prioritization
External	Internal

Figure 2: Minimalism in comparison to Consumerism

Financial gurus, minimalists, and others often quote this succinct observational quote that Robert Quillen made: "We purchase things we don't want, with money which we don't own, to impress those we don't love." Sometimes, we don't even have the right people to impress.

Minimalism can reverse the downward spiral in consumerism. A consumerist mindset assigns meanings and uses tools and means. Money and material possessions serve a purpose, but are not the ultimate goal. We consume these as if they were the most important things in our lives. When we adopt a minimalist mindset, it is easy to remember what the most important things are in life.

Antoine de Saint Exupery's 1943 novel The Little Prince wrote that only the heart can see the truth. What is essential is not visible to the eye.

Minimalism lets you go deep. It allows us to do a heartcheck. Then, with renewed eyes, we can look out at our world and scan the items we have created. We ask ourselves, "Do I really need this?" Is it something my heart truly wants? What purpose does it have in my life? Why am I so attached to it? Why am I so attached to this? Are my motivators positive? Or is it rooted fear, anxiety, or insecurity? What would happen to it if I let go?

The most popular anecdote focuses on prioritizing essentials. Here is a slightly modified version.

A professor sets an empty jar at the table for his class. He carefully inserts his valuable gold shells with pearls inside and asks his students if the jar has been filled. His class responds yes.

Then, he places some pebbles inside the jar to fill the spaces between the shells of gold. He then asks the class if their jars are full. They say yes.

Then, he pours sand inside the jar filling the small spaces between the golden shells and pebbles. He then asks his classmates if the jar has reached its full capacity. They answered with a resounding YES

He pours water from his sea into the jar. The jar is then soaked up. He declares the container full.

He then explained to his class that the jar is a symbol of life, while the gold shells and pearls represent the priority areas in one's life: relationships and health. Your jar will still have the richness and fullness of saltwater, sand, pebbles.

The tools or enablers of the pebbles are they. They support the golden shells. These are material things like your job and house, your clothing, and your net worth. These could also include tools, such as education and minimalism.

Sand is all the small things. If you pour the sand first, you won't have room for the pebbles or gold shells. If you start with the pebbles, the space will be too small for the golden shells. Prioritize gold shells first. Next, let pebbles be second.

One of his students questions the meaning of saltwater. The professor smiles, and responds: "No mater how full your life seems, there's always time and space for you to enjoy the ocean with your loved ones."

Ask yourself: What is your golden shell? What are your most important items? How are you handling your gold shells and jewelry? Who are your pearls, and how do you feel about them? What are you most proud of in your life?

If you're putting too much emphasis on saltwater or sand, then it may be time to review your priorities. The accumulation of pebbles is only part of life. It is all about how well the pebbles fit inside your jar, between your pearls and your gold shells.

Consumerism involves a jar filled only with pebbles, saltwater, and sand. Minimalism means that you empty the jar and then put all of your gold shells in their correct places.

This leads to the functional definition minimalism being prioritization.

Minimalism makes it possible to use resources in a thoughtful and efficient manner.

Individuals and groups need to manage these three resources. These are time, energy, and money.

Figure 3: Three Resources of Individuals and Groups in Project Management Triangle

For managers, growth in a business or corporation means maximizing or saving time, money, energy, and other resources. This is how companies create more goods and more services. This is how consumerism can be sustained.

We can all save our time, money, energy and be more efficient as individuals if minimalism is practiced.

Examine your life right now. Which aspects of your life are you feeling extravagant? Do you work too hard to make enough money to buy what you need? Are you working to pay off debts which keep growing regardless of how much you make? Do you spend too much on whims, sales or vices to fund an addiction? Are you spending too much time driving to work or commuting for hours each day? Do you spend too much of your time watching television and scrolling through social media news feeds right before bed?

How do I channel my finite resources (times, money and energy) into more productive activities or into activities that make my heart sing and dance, rather than scream, sag, and scream?

When was the most recent time you spent some time at the beach or on the sea, basking and enjoying a relaxing moment with your family or close friends?

These are all reflection points you can reflect upon when you start your journey toward minimalism.

Minimalism pushes you towards setting a personal intention to create more space for the necessities, and to manage your resources carefully. This helps to eliminate the influence of consumerism in the life of the individual and gives you a sense that your happiness and fulfillment are not dependent on the material world.

But, you don't wish to one day be a full-fledged minimalist. You will continue this journey throughout your life. This brings us to minimalism as a way for living.

Minimalism is how you live your day.

Minimalism doesn't happen overnight. It's a mentality that you choose and a way that you choose live every day.

Let's return to the analogies that we used earlier to understand this principle better.

When you commit to living a healthy lifestyle you will never stop striving for it. It is essential to continue it. It is possible to have setbacks and eat processed foods from time-to-time, but it is not necessary for you to go back to your old ways. You can keep living a healthy lifestyle and you must continue to move forward.

When you commit to managing your finances with care, you will not stop until you reach your goal of becoming a millionaire. You have to maintain it. You risk losing your millions and falling back on your old ways.

As a parent to children, your role doesn't end when they finish school, graduate, marry and start their own families. Your role as parent can change depending on your children's life stages. However, you will remain their parent every day and throughout their lives.

You can also set an intention to be minimalist and put your focus on the basics. Then you'll choose to make minimalism your daily habit.

It's like a habit you form and build. Minimalists will never give up on minimalism. They just become more comfortable with it. They don't just wake up and declare that they are the master minimalist and cease to be minimalists. They persevere in their efforts and keep moving forward. They choose minimalism and live it every day.

Are you ready?

Chapter 18: Minimalism in Your Daily Life

Be as simple as you can, but not more complicated. --paraphrased maxim from Albert Einstein

Minimalism does NOT mean that you should not own anything. That you shouldn't own anything is minimalism. --Joshua Becker - writer and minimalist

How are you feeling right now? Consider yesterday. What do you think about your future outlook? Do you have a positive outlook or are you frightened? Do you feel happy with all aspects of your life?

Now, let me ask you a few more questions. Now, look within and answer honestly.

Examine Different Aspects of Daily Life

Do you feel that you lack time for your health and family? Are you constantly multi-tasking and rushing?

Do you drag your self to work every single day? Are you dependent on coffee and sleeping pills for your mornings? Are you feeling stressed and overwhelmed?

Are you required or permitted to attend tedious, long-winding meetings that never seem productive? Are there folders covering your computer screen, making it difficult to retrieve files from your bosses or colleagues? Are you surrounded by clutter at work? Do you struggle to complete real work because of all the paperwork you handle? Do you gossip or engage in unnecessary conversations?

Do you commute too much to and from work? Or do you prefer to stay close to home to find work?

Are you busy, but not feeling like you are growing? Do you feel stuck? Do you feel life is meaningless?

Do you have dishes in your sink that you are too lazy or too busy to wash? You might have all your utensils in the dishwasher, but you are too busy to load them. Do you have too much plates, cups and glasses? Are there so many spoons and forks in your dishwasher that you can't even clean the sink?

Did you ever find yourself staring at your full wardrobe and not finding anything to wear it? Do you spend hours every single day dressing up? Do you remember being late for work or missing an appointment because you spent so much time looking for the right clothing?

Do you feel anxious about inviting friends to your home or hosting unexpected visitors? Are you having trouble finding things in your space?

Do you feel anxious just thinking about cleaning your house? Are your tables and chairs cluttered? You might consider cleaning them up by placing a fancy blanket above the chairs and tables.

What are your finances like? Are you living paycheck-to-paycheck? Are you having trouble managing your finances? Are you drowning because of your debt? Are you someone who makes a budget and doesn't follow it? Do you try to keep to your budget every time you make it but forget to do so when you find a good deal? You think it makes sense to purchase something with your credit cards, even if there isn't enough money right now.

Are you paying off loans, mortgages, or other debts with a large portion of your salary? You might find that your hard-earned dollars are being used for car and/or home maintenance. Perhaps you have vices or addictive behaviors that require you to spend large sums of money.

Do you have a project in your life that you want to finish but keep putting off until it is too late? Do you procrastinate because you are too busy?

Do you long to be your own boss, but feel uncomfortable or difficult working for someone else? You have resigned to working for someone else, even if it's a horrible job, until you turn 60.

Do you need a lot of large luggage to travel? Do you spend most of your vacation time shopping for trinkets or food? Are you willing to pay extra for baggage and trinkets when you get back home?

Do you find it difficult to let things go because of their sentimental worth? Do you find it difficult to let go of sentimental items? Or do your feelings of regret and emptiness immediately after letting go?

Although I have many questions that I am familiar with, if at least one of them was answered, it's a good sign that you have read this entire book. I urge you not to stop reading. You can think back to the questions that best describe you. As you read the books, you will be able to examine this part of your own life.

It's time for you simplify your life. It's time to regain control and manage your time. You have the opportunity to redirect your energy into making you happy and satisfied.

Minimalism can have a positive impact on daily life

You can do this by exploring the many benefits of minimalism in daily life. Minimalism lets you focus on what matters most, and removes you from the attachment to material possessions.

It takes you out of the grips of consumerism. It makes it possible to be grateful for what you do have.

It takes away your anxiety from the past, past and future. Instead, you can live in the present with gratitude and hope for what lies ahead. It opens up your potential and makes it possible to produce more and consume less. You can also contribute to the society you live in. At its best, minimalism inspires others.

Below is a summary of the key features of minimalism in relation to consumerism.

Consumerism   Minimalism

The outer world can be grown   Your inner world can be developed

Accumulate, attach, possess, own Get   free from the chains of slavery, be committed, then liberate

There is no such thing as enough discontent   Content is enough

Resent, devalue   Thank, appreciate

Time-consuming   Time-maximizing

Still stuck in the past   Live in the now

Uncertain about the future

Work hard to achieve status, a stable career, and financial gain   Love the work you do

Productive work

Pursue passion

Discover mission

Live with purpose

Shopping around? Buy and Consume
Make, produce, and contribute

Figure 4: Comparison of Materialism and Consumerism

Minimalism can be a mindset that helps you simplify all aspects in your life. If you use minimalism daily in all aspects your life, you will reap the benefits beyond the features.

Better health. It helps you focus on your health and is more in touch with your mind and body. It reduces stress-related health problems and helps to manage stress more effectively.

Personal growth. When you look within, you can expand your inner world. You are able to realize your potential. You plant seeds and then watch them bear fruit.

More space. Decluttering is a process of getting rid of items that don't serve your highest purpose. This allows you to have more space. It is attractive and makes your home look more spacious. You'll save time and don't spend hours looking through your clutter. It's easier to organize your clutter. You have literally space to entertain guests, invited or uninvited. It is easier to clean up and save energy. You might also save money if your items are sold to bless those in need.

Take control of your finances. A simplified lifestyle will help you manage your finances better. You can manage your finances better by creating a solid budget.

Find work you love. You don't have to be satisfied with a job that is stable and pays a regular income. However, it can hinder your ability to fulfill your true dreams. Maybe this is why minimalists eventually decide to work less for others, and instead work for themselves. It's much easier for them to manage their energy and time. Entrepreneurship might not be for everyone. It is your decision. It's about finding your own calling.

More time and energy. You might find this ironic. The time we have is limited. We all have 24 hour days, 7 day a week, and 365 days in a year. If it's leap year, 366 days. This constant is true regardless of your time zone. We should recognize that time is a binder, even though it may be measured in seconds, minutes or hours. We are limited in time. We do not live forever. Why is it that some people seem to have more free time? The secret to their success is making time for what they need. Corporations and businesses need to be able to manage their time. This is also a benefit for individuals. Minimalism can help here.

By reducing the number of aspects in your life, you will discover that there is no shortage or excess time. You find that you have enough to do all the things you love: rest, work, eat, pray and love. You find that it doesn't matter if you don't answer that urgent email while having dinner. You'll be happier sharing stories with your loved ones while you eat dinner together than when you spend your time on your smartphones. If you make it easier to organize your wardrobe and dresser, you'll find that you have more free time in the morning for meditation or cooking breakfast for your family. This will allow you to spend more time with your guests, rather than spending hours tidying up your clutter.

Less baggage. Minimalists are known to travel light. When they travel or go to places, minimalists often only have one bag. They can travel more easily because they don't have to carry as much luggage. They can also save on their check-in luggage and avoid the frustration of losing their luggage. It keeps them moving and on their toes. Milan Kundera wrote that there is also a "lightness of being". It is possible to go through your day without feeling overwhelmed by debt, clutter, stress, resentments and other negative emotions.

Environment-conscious. Many minimalists use environment-friendly methods. They do not just ensure that the purchase is necessary; they also make sure that the product or service they are purchasing is responsibly sourced, manufactured and sold. They prefer products that are not harmful for the environment. They value superior quality and prefer to make long-term purchases that will not be thrown away. They will not buy something out of habit, on a whim or because it is cheap, fancy or if an upscale friend recommends it. They are very concerned about how products and services are made. They look for products and brands that have environment-conscious and sustainable practices. Some people even set themselves the goal of reducing their carbon footprint.

Do it for others. Minimalism inspires people. It is an example for children. It is aware of the importance of ensuring that future generations have access to the limited resources of the planet.

It takes small daily changes to make a lasting lifestyle that can help improve your life, and inspire others.

Chapter 19: Mindset Changes, Finding Balance

The intention of voluntary simplicity does not mean to live in a vacuum. It is the more difficult goal of living with balance. This is a middle-way that moves between the extremes poverty and indulgence. --Duane Elgin, media activist

For years, I believed I should be more organized. Now I understand that I only needed less stuff. --Alysa Baijenaru is a blogger and dietitian.

Let us look at the advantages and features of minimalism using stories from three people. These 3 stories give life to the idea of minimalism.

Conner's story: From consumeristic to conscious

Conner exudes success. Conner grew up in a middle-class home and was taught that hard work is the key to success. He must finish his studies with high honors and work for a multinational corporation to reach the top.

He did it by working hard. He graduated at the top in his class, worked for an insurance company, and within four years was promoted to the position of category manager. He is that good.

Conner was able quickly to repay his student loans. Conner bought a huge house for himself as well his parents. He also purchased a luxury car and home for his younger brother. He eats out nearly every night at restaurants. He is a member of expensive gyms and clubs. Mina is his girlfriend from college and he maintains a good relationship with her. His coworkers and graduate students love him.

But deep down, he senses something is wrong. Sometimes he feels stressed and not relaxed. He feels overwhelmed with the amount of appointments and engagements for the day, sometimes while driving. It's as if he is on a reality-show called Keeping up with Conner.

It doesn't help his credit card debt, which is growing alongside his mortgage payment and car loan payment, that keeps him from getting more. His salary increases each year. He receives quarterly bonuses based on the performance of his employees and the performance the company. His college peers earn 20 times his salary. However, this is not enough. His lifestyle and purchases grow along with his income. There is something inside that urges him to change some aspect of his life. He was just too busy and distracted to hear that inner voice.

Mina noticed that Mina was feeling too stressed in the last days and suggested they go on vacation. He instantly booked a weeklong stay at a Caribbean resort. Conner had to go to work every night, so it was a lovely and relaxing vacation. He was always checking his mobile phone while out on the boat. Although he was island-hopping, it appears he was also mind-hopping.

It was back to normal when they got back home. Conner was still feeling full. Mina introduced Conner, Joshua, and Ryan to Mina. They shared their minimalist lifestyle and their 21-day journey to minimalism.

Conner went through a 3-month transformation program that included Ryan, Joshua, Mina and Joshua. Conner simply modified his mindset and changed his lifestyle. He took small steps every day until minimalism became a routine or a common thing to him. Finally, he began to breathe minimalism.

He cleared his house. He donated or sold all furniture, appliances and clothing he no longer needed after two weeks. He disposed off items that were not working. He eventually sold his big house after 3 months and moved into one main room in the large house he purchased for parents.

He also decluttered the car by throwing out old receipts, empty bottles, and any other junk that had accumulated over the years. He also discovered coins and bills in the trunk. He eventually sold the car. He purchased a basic motorcycle instead. He has always longed for the freedom of riding a bike from one city to another.

Because he was passionate about his work, he decided to stay in his office job. He let go all the technical details. He began delegating more of his tasks to his coworkers. He realized that he had been taking on more work than could be done by his coworkers. He found that juniors can perform certain managerial tasks. Sometimes they surpass his expectations. He could be a good mentor and manage his time more effectively.

He also reviewed his finances and devised a budget. He allocated percentages for debt settlement and savings, investments as well as daily expenses, recreation, contribution, the future and retirement. He also made a fortune by selling unwanted stuff. These proceeds were donated to his alma matter's scholarship fund.

He now focuses on his overall health. Instead of going to the fitness center almost every day, his focus now is on holistic health. It's not only about exercise; it's about nutrition, rest, and nutrition. As a result, he eats healthier and more homecooked meals, sleeps for 6 hours instead of 2 and works out for 15 minutes every day rather than spending 2 hours in the gym.

He also spends many hours cooking weekends with his girlfriend and parents to prepare and cook meals for the coming week. He discovered his culinary skills and that cooking is something he really enjoys. He surprised his colleagues at work one day by bringing in a delicious beef stew and dark chocolate brownies.

They were surprised that he had cooked and baked the goodies. While chewing the brownies his boss said, "Conner, can you do anything?" To which he replied with a joke: "Yes. I can't quit being so good at it." They shared a good laugh over the beef stew.

He is now happier and more energetic after 3 months. His confidence comes from within, and not from material purchases.

Conner discovered many things during the transition. He discovered that he doesn't really need anything more. He discovered that his relationships were more important than anything. He spends more with his parents now. He cooks for them and enjoys their dinners.

Mina also surprised him and continued to support him despite his mood swings. This minimalist lifestyle was a blessing that he will never forget. She made a huge impact on his life and will change it forever. He is so grateful for her positive influence in his lives. He also loves the positive energy she radiates wherever she goes. He proposed to her last year and they plan to marry next year. They would prefer to keep the wedding intimate and simple than have a large one.

Stan, his brother, is going to be his best man for the wedding. Conner and he are now in week one. Their brotherly bond has turned into minimalism.

Conner's inspirational journey is both heartwarming and inspiring, don't ya think?

The Story Of Dea: Detached or Dynamic?

Dea too exudes success, much like Conner. She comes from a middle class family. She has five sisters, who shared her room until they moved out of home to go to college.

Her mother and her parents were both very much into saving for the rainy day. They were thrifty. Her father keeps a lot of discount coupons. His mother, along with other trinkets like tissues and condiment packets from restaurants keeps a selection of coupons.

Their house was full clutter. Their living area was full of family pictures. Her mother seems always to be cooking. She loves to cook. Dea and her siblings were the ones she shared a love for cooking and food.

The family was always full of laughter. It was full of visitors and neighbours who came and went to enjoy the homemade and delicious meals and snacks prepared by her mom. They did not mind clutter. They would simply throw a pillow over the couch if they couldn't find a suitable place to sleep.

She learned how to complete assignments, study, and write papers in the midst of all this chaos and chatter. However, deep down she longs for simplicity and calm space.

When she left home to go to college, she chose a small apartment for her and not a large dorm that had many other students. She started working in a design business after graduating with high honors. Her style was clean and minimalist. Clients and bosses love her elegant and simple outputs.

She currently lives in an apartment with a large kitchenette. When her siblings and parents visit her, they often comment on how monkish-like and austere her living area is. They would repeatedly say "It seems like nobody is living there!" She keeps a well-stocked kitchen and cooks often. She also practice yoga daily. Her wardrobe is vast. She owns hundreds of clothes in neutral or light pastel colors. She may have 3 to 4 pieces of the identical clothing. Her shoe collection is impeccable.

She has few close friends from college or at work. Although she is close to her family, she still has many close friends from her childhood. She only visits them once a holiday.

At 25, she still doesn't have a boyfriend. She's had some casual flings, but nothing more serious. She yearns to travel but lacks the drive and motivation to do so. She once planned a trip. She searched for places and plotted her budget and itineraries using Excel. But she lost track of it.

People mistakenly believe that she is wealthy due to her elegant style and simple life. She doesn't have any savings, and she also has credit card debt. This is because she enjoys buying high-end, quality items. She buys many pieces when she finds something that she likes.

She feels like something is missing when she meditates after her daily yoga practice or drives home from work. Or, perhaps, while enjoying a delicious meal she has just prepared. She has achieved something for her: her own place, a space without clutter and a steady job she enjoys. However, she feels like it is not enough. She doesn't feel enough. She feels too empty and detached inside. She went about her daily life as usual, not paying much attention to the voice inside.

Her boss then asked her to give a design pitch to potential clients from a pharmaceutical firm. Conner, a senior man in the crowd, had a quiet and calm demeanour that attracted her to his presentation. He is the boss of that company. His words are precise, well thought out and thoughtfully spoken when he speaks. His colleagues listen when he speaks. He is calm but authoritative. He looks like a wiseman.

They won the pitch. The account was opened and she worked closely together with Conner the vice president. Conner introduced Dea to Mina, his wife of 15 year, and they became friends. Dea asked Conner & Mina during one of their dinners what their secret is because they seem so happy & fulfilled in their lives.

"We keep life simple," they all agreed. Dea was introduced to the idea of minimalism. Dea seemed to be minimalistic and they thought Dea was aware of it. They were surprised when Dea revealed her entire life. Dea and her husband were both in tears. Dea was in tears when she realized the extent her detachedness after confiding to someone else. Conner and Mina were in tears as they realized that Dea has so many more things than she knows.

Together they devised Dea's journey towards minimalism. Conner, Mina and Dea encouraged Dea take a moment to examine her life from her relationships to her finances.

Dea didn't need to clear out as much as she had already done. When she looked at her pantry and wardrobe, she saw that she has excess. Similar pairs of her staple clothing items are unworn and still have price tags. She sold some of her clothes and gave some to her parents and siblings. Most of her herbs and spices that she kept in the kitchen cabinets were now old, some even had molds. She decided to throw the contents out and recycle the containers.

Slowly, her living space was given a personal touch. She took all of the designs and paintings she had created over the years and unrolled them. Then, she framed them and put them up on the walls. When her parents saw the wall decorations, they gasped and admired them. She proudly claimed that she made them. She promised to make one for each of them as a surprise. Conner and Mina were delighted to see her painting and placed it in their living room.

She also made plans for her college friends to travel. She now visits her parents at least quarterly. Her childhood friends are her best friends. She makes it a point never to make small talk with them. A local entrepreneur is the man she's now seeing, someone she found while wandering through an art gallery near her parents. She's taking her sweet time getting to know this man.

Tom Pappalardo, graphic designer, stated that there is a fine line between minimalism (and not trying very hard)

Dea finally found the essence of minimalism. She has finally found the level minimalism that works for her and makes her happy.

Dea was reading Harukimurakami one day and a line caught her eye: "Once it's clear that you want to get rid of something you cannot discard it." Not very much. You can get rid almost anything if you set your mind to it. It's easy to want to get rid off everything when you start to throw things out. It's almost like you have gambled away all your money and decided that it was time to get rid of everything. Too much trouble to keep the rest."

She realized that her old self was similar to this. She was melancholy and recalled how easy she had let go of her material possessions. She felt lost and alone without an inner anchor. It is not enough to improve the outer world. Minimalism was her vehicle to travel to her inner realm to find her motivators, and demotivators. This allowed her to uncover her true desires. It made things more manageable. It changed her perspective and gave her the ability to set goals.

Comparing Conner & Dea

Before we continue with the third story, allow us to briefly compare Conner & Dea. They were both raised in extreme consumerism and detachedness.

Let us return to the minimalism scale/spectrum. However, this time, let's think of it more as a seesaw, or balance beam.

As you can clearly see, there's a fulcrum which balances the beam or lever. This triangle fulcrum is where you set your intention, your vision and your motivator. These are your goldshells. This is your golden shell. It's what keeps you going, what motivates you, what helps you see the bigger picture, what gives your life meaning, what gives your heart joy, and what makes you dance with joy and live your best life.

The lever must have the fulcrum at the center of it in order to balance. The triangle's long base must be located at the bottom to ensure it is grounded. It is much more difficult for the beam to balance if it is at its bottom.

Also, your intention and mindset must not be upside-down. Your motivations should be positive. It will be difficult to balance if the beam is focused on negative, upside-down or other worldly desires. It is not stable. It can be easily tossed around. It is easy to slide to the extreme ends if it isn't grounded.

Let's take a look at the balancing light Conner and Dea had before they began their journey toward minimalism.

Conner is a balance beam who leans towards consumerism. Conner has his fulcrum reversed. He is more concerned with material acquisition.

Dea's balance beam is on the right side for detachment. Her fulcrum also appears reversed. She focuses too heavily on the outside and neglects to do anything meaningful for her inside space.

First, reverse the triangle-fulcrum. Conner and Dea both did this. After they had woken up from their sleep for the last time, Conner and Dea looked inside to discover their fulcrum (or their heart's centre).

They moved the corrected beam's fulcrum towards the center, to achieve more balance in the lives of their loved ones.

Now that we have an in-depth understanding of how minimalism can balance the beam, let's now move on to the third story.

Your Journey into Minimalism: The Story of You

So, what is the third story?

Yours, of course!

What's your story? How do you want to see your story continue and grow?

What is it that motivated you to get this book and begin reading it? What is your fulcrum. Is it negative or positive? Is there a way to change it and make it positive? What is your heart telling?

What level of minimalism are you aiming to achieve? Where do you want minimalism to be implemented? How can minimalism be implemented in your daily life

How did you feel about minimalism prior to reading this book. Now, how about this?

Are all these questions making you uncomfortable? Do these questions make you feel uncomfortable? Good. Because you won't grow being in your comfort zone. Change is difficult. Change is hard. Because there's no other option than to keep moving forward. When you awaken it is difficult to go back to bed, knowing that you must move forward. Shia LaBeouf, the actor, spoke of repeatedly reminding us to do it.

"Do it. Do it. Don't let your dreams be dreams. Yesterday was tomorrow. You just have to do it. Let your dreams become a reality. It's possible. People dream of success while you'll be working hard. Nothing is impossible. You shouldn't quit until you reach the place where others would. Don't wait! Do it. Don't hesitate to do it. Yes you can. It's possible. You don't have to give up if it makes you tired.

It is about taking the first step now. It starts by having a new mindset and setting the right fulcrum for your intention.

Chapter 20: How to Apply Your Life Gradually

It is important to not only focus on success, but also on significance. If you do this, even the small wins along your way will become more meaningful. Oprah Winfrey (talk show host, philanthropist).

The first chapter introduced the concept/scale of minimalism. We built on that imagery in the second chapter and introduced the concept of minimalism, either as a balance beam or seesaw. These models and concepts are backed by faces. Conner, Dea and others showed us what it is like to be at the extremes. They shared their journey to minimalism as an inspiration and guideline for others.

We'll summarize the guidelines in this chapter and give more tips and pointers. These guidelines, pointsers, and tips should be considered as simple road signage.

If you're walking along this cobbled path known as minimalism, you might notice a tip or road sign that says "Turn right for vegetarianism." You don't have any obligation to follow this signage to the right unless you want to go that route and become a vegetarian. If you do not understand the sign, continue on your journey. With the knowledge and understanding of minimalism, some people can find the way to vegetarianism.

Another example is that you may be driving along the highway known as minimalism together with your spouse or baby twins. You might see a road sign that says "Get rid of all attachments and clinging on to things and places." Your wife may not want to abandon her car and walk the length of the highway, carrying a baby. It doesn't matter if you follow this signage or abandon your family.

You have the option to just carry on as normal, understanding that some people (perhaps solo backpackers) will not be able to ignore this sign. You can continue on your journey, knowing that your family is your most important asset and that your car will transport you to your destination, but you also have the option to be at peace.

Your inability to follow the signage and take that route does not mean you are a lesser minimalist. Similar to your situation, others who did follow the signage do not have any superiority or inferiority. Minimalism means to forgo comparisons that encourage envy, gloating or other negative emotions.

This caveat being said, let's move on to minimalism. These practical steps will assist you in taking that first step, finding the balance you need, and then finding what works for your needs.

Road Tip # 1. Make minimalism a habit.

Ryan Nicodemus (Ryan Nicodemus) and Joshua Fields Millburn shared their journey to minimalism over 21 days. This is based in popular psychology's idea that it takes 21 day to make a habit. However, Jeremy Dean, a psychologist, found that it takes 66 days for a habit to become a permanent one.

It takes up to three weeks to create a habit that you can sustain and makes it part of your daily schedule. However, it can take up 3 months for it to become second nature.

You can make minimalism a daily habit by planning not only for one day, but also for a week. It means to plan in phases.

Joshua and Ryan can be your guide and help you plan minimalism activities for your first 21 days. Joshua introduced Ryan the concept of minimalism. Ryan was to follow Joshua's example and plan his journey according to this list.

They began the journey by taking 2 days to reflect, then followed by one week of action. Ryan and Joshua invited Joshua, Joshua's dad, and his girlfriend, to "packing parties".

Then, over the next seven days, he only unpacked what he was going to use that day. He began to unpack essentials such toiletries, clothes, and kitchen utensils. Ryan kept going until Day 10 when he realized that there was no need to pack anything for the day. The next four days were allotted for reviewing the remaining unpacked items. He made the final decision on whether each item should be donated, sold, digitized, or disposed of.

He found that his house now has more space after the decluttering. He felt more organized and clearer and began to look at other areas of life.

Ryan's journey began this way. He did not give up after 21 days. He kept the minimalist lifestyle going for 3 months after this preparatory period. Joshua helped him create a minimalist website that he shared with others, to help them discover their own paths of minimalism.

How would your first 21 days on your minimalism journey look? What areas in your life can you benefit from a minimalist approach

How would you plan your next 45-days to make sure you don't fall back into the old ways? How can sustainability be achieved and how do you embed the habit of minimalism in your life? Take a look at this. You can plan and decide what you want to do, and then make it a reality.

Road Tip # 2 - Find joy, balance and peace from a positive centre.

In the previous chapter, we mentioned how the fulcrum needs to be grounded, and not upside-down. This is because an upside-down fullcrum can cause the beam's topple.

Find a positive motivator and follow the same steps. What drives you? What drives you?

You may be tempted to continue on the path of minimalism if you find yourself filled with envy, spite, resentment anger, hatred loneliness, and other negative emotions. It might be worth looking for a better trigger or driver. What can you do to channel your anger and frustration into passion, envy and resentment in gratitude, hatred into love, loneliness into reaching out to people, and your hatred into compassion?

Let's get back to Dea. Dea was a minimalist, but she felt empty. While she was able to let go and enjoy minimalism, she felt empty inside. She needed to awaken to the fact that space is not an end goal. Instead, space should be used to create happy relationships and bring joy to others.

Arlene's story is another example. She recently separated from her husband of 15-years. He married a younger woman that he met at his job and left her. She was awarded custody of their twins, who are now attending college. She is still racked with anger and hurt from the split, but her sons are there to support her. They know she will be an empty nester soon, and don't want to see her become depressed or lonely. They encouraged her find other distractions.

One morning they woke to find her unusually happy and throwing away stuff her husband had left behind. She regretted the fact that she had thrown away so much of her stuff. He's no longer her husband. But he was her husband. She realized that she was trying throw away 15 years worth of their marriage when she sold all his possessions. But, it wasn't just his presence she had to give away.

All of these things had been removed, and she was left feeling empty and alone. It was as if she had lost her anchor. It is as if she has lost a small part of herself. It wasn't enough just to get rid of clutter and toss it away. She needs more awareness of the things she throws at her, literally and metaphorically.

She was able to go through therapy, join community organizations, as well as rekindle her love for writing, knitting, and other creative pursuits. After her sons went off to college, she decided to live in a smaller home near her siblings and their families. This is convenient as it is only 2 cities away from their university.

Arlene's story may not be your story, but it is possible to find inspiration in her story to make heartbreak a chance to transform your life.

It's not all about seeing life through rose-colored eyes or being optimistic. It's about turning a negative situation into a positive, turning an obstacle or problem into a solution, turning brokenness in to a chance for healing, and turning pain back into transformation.

Kintsugi (Japanese method) is a Japanese way to fix broken pottery. This involves using liquid lacquer that has been mixed with gold or silver and other precious metals. Beautiful patterns can be found in the resurrected pottery. It's almost like giving new life or purpose to things that are broken.

Figure 10: Gold is used to repair broken pottery

This is a good image to illustrate minimalism. Minimalism is a liquid lacquer that can put your life back together. It's especially useful if you feel like your life is in chaos or fragments.

People marvel at the gold and silver lacquer when they see kintsugi ceramic. But the potter knows it's not all about the lacquer. It's not even about the pot. It's not about the pot.

People often marvel at the minimalist's decluttered life and how everything is in its place. But minimalism isn't about these tangibles. It's not minimalistism and minimalist practices. It is about minimalism as a vehicle for containing "goldshells" or the blessings of your life.

Minimalism can be fueled by appreciation, constructive, and positive feelings. Positive thoughts, feelings and attitudes are like kintsugi who appreciates the cup of coffee and repairs it. Negative emotions and thoughts are just as destructive as throwing the broken cup away.

So, what is your motivation to pursue minimalism?

Road Tip #3: There are many forms and applications of minimalism. Take care.

There are many ways to cook eggs. Just know what you like. If you do not like eggs, find a substitute metaphor. Minimalism is the same. It is a dynamic process. There are many ways to approach it. You can just pick the ones that will work best for your situation. You can approach it any way you want. You can start in any area of your life. Here are some suggestions to help you jumpstart your career.

- Declutter your space. Sort and then sell, digitize, or dispose.

- Manage your finances (budget).

- Manage time (schedule)

Manage your nutrition, health, and exercise

- Make it a habit to be in relationships, spend more time with family and friends.

Rediscover or redirect energy, purpose and mission in your life.

Decluttering is the most important step in minimalism. Because it's the easiest thing to do among the ones listed above, You can see the immediate and tangible results, which are motivating enough to keep going.

Minimalist living is like practicing yoga in a way. One of the most common posters found in yoga studios states that "Yoga's not for the flexible". It's only for the willing." The same goes for minimalism. It's for those who are willing.

Many people start yoga by not being able or able to touch their toes. Many yoga students end their first yoga class by lying down in savasana, a resting posture, and pleading for breath. With consistent practice, they begin to notice an improvement in flexibility. They can now fold gracefully from their hips and lay flat on the ground with ease. They can better control their breathing. They will find their favorite position, the one that feels comfortable and natural for them. Then, they can master more difficult postures. Each person's body is unique. It is possible for amateurs to find a pose they like, even if it is not something that long-standing yoga practitioners are able to do.

All you have to do is decide to do it. Then, actually do it. It works the same way with minimalism, and all other decisions in life.

Claire Dederer describes her journey to find her pose in Poser: My Life In Twenty-Three Yoga Poses. Claire tells us how she did her first garudasana (eagle pose)

"I caught sight in the mirror of myself. I felt totally at ease in this post, yet I looked completely unlike me.

I discovered that there was joy in being something new. You could force yourself to be a new shape. It was just a matter of finding the right way to do it in my own life.

Ryan began his 21-day journey to minimalism in a parallel reality. He realized how many possessions he had. But at the end it was his best friends, his father and his girlfriend that mattered most. After decluttering his house successfully, Ryan moved into his car to start focusing on other aspects of life.

Just take one thing at a given time. Focus on one aspect at once, one pose at one time, and one day at one. Then you'll see how minimalism transformed that area of life. How that pose became your favorite. How it changed the direction you live in. That eureka moment fuels you and is a sign of what you're doing right. With the increased confidence and understanding you gain, it is your signal that you are ready to tackle another part of your life.

These are some ideas to help you live a minimalist lifestyle. Which one is right for you? These are just signs along the road. You have to decide which path you take. If you do not feel it is the right path for you, then you do not have to continue on. Explore, try, and continue moving.

Pack-Unpack

Like Joshua did, plan a packing party. You should pack everything as if it were your move away. All of your belongings, including your television, fridge, freezer, appliances, toiletries towels, wardrobe, and everything else, must be packed. Put everything you have in one room. Cover large items such as the fridge and bed with a blanket.

Then, take 7 days to unpack everything you use for each day. After 7 days go through everything you didn't unpack. Sort them into 5 buckets.

- Donate. Do you own duplicates, or triplicates of any televisions? Do you own more televisions than one? Do you own three pieces of the exact same blouse? Donate repeating items. Donate items you don't use very often, don't use anymore, and don't even use. Do you know of any institutions or individuals who could benefit? Ask your colleagues and friends. Seek out charitable institutions that are truly helping people.

- Sell. You can choose to sell the extra TV, the suit you bought, or that beautiful painting that has been sitting in your attic. You have two options: sell it in your garage or online. It is important to set a time frame. If the item doesn't sell in 7 or 14 business days, you can donate it.

- Digitize. Scan, take photos or create softcopies of hard copies. This applies to documents, receipts and photos as well letters and other memorabilia. Rip CDs, DVDs. For backup, combine files from several storage devices into one device (hard drive) and into 1 cloud storage.

Once you have made digital copies of your documents, you can shred receipts as well as unimportant papers and dispose of the paper in junk shops. All important documents should be kept in one folder or safebox. Donate or sell your CDs and DVDs. Flash disks can be rewritten and other storage devices may also be rewritten. Keep only what you really need. Then, give the extra storage devices back to your office or to students in your family who might be in need of flash disks.

- Repurpose. You can place photos, letters and memorabilia at a central spot in your home. Perhaps you want to show off your artistic skills by framing and making decorations from these sentimental items. Create a beautiful album, portrait collage, magnet, or ref magnet of family pictures to gift your parents or siblings.

You might have a collection you don't want to part with. Perhaps you have a large collection of coins that is too valuable to be given away. Or maybe you have a collection drawings that are too precious to be thrown away. Keep them. But why not make good use of them? They can be displayed in your living room, bedroom, or office.

- Dispose. Get rid of everything you don't use. You must dispose of the items correctly. Your trash can be divided into biodegradable or non-biodegradable categories. Perhaps you can sort them by types such as plastics or paper.

Is your pantry stuffed with expired bottles, cans, and condiments These items should not be thrown away with damp or tattered clothing, damp rags, and dead plants. You can help your community garbage collector by separating your trash.

Have you ever had a device that stopped working? Are there multiple batteries or chargers? Dispose electronics properly. There are institutions that will collect electronics for proper disposal and recycling.

This pack and unpack method is great for singles who live alone. It may be difficult for large families to do this, but it is possible. Over the weekend, it can be great to have fun with your children by hosting a packing party or selling at garage sales. It can be very difficult to let go some things, especially sentimental baby clothes and toys. However, remember that the family who cleans together stays together.

One item at the time, One Cabinet at the Time

You don't need to pack-unpack if this is not what you are looking for or it is not feasible due to your schedule or family size. There are other ways of clearing clutter.

Take on a minimalist challenge. Get rid of all the things you haven't used for a while. You can dispose of one item each day and choose to either donate, sell or dispose. People start with their pantry, medicine cabinet, and wardrobe.

Another option is to hack your cabinet. Or, you could place all your clothes one side of the cupboard and your hangers the other. If you do not change your routine every day for a month, you will end up with clothes you never wear. There may be clothes that you tried on but didn't end up wearing, or they don't suit you. You could put the pile of unwanted or unused clothes in the drawer to the side. Hang them the other way. It's important to distinguish what you use from the things you don't, what you need from what else. After one month, throw out the unneeded and unwanted.

The same applies to your pantry. Keep only condiments and goods you actually use. Toss away any medicines or goods that are no longer in use. Refrigerate your refrigerator. You should label containers clearly so you don't end with containers with an unknown expiration or contents. Do not stack too much.

Slowly work through these steps. Start with the easiest aspect and move on. You will experience discomfort at first, but you will soon feel lighter and more free when you let go.

A quote from an unknown source states, "If it doesn't nourish you soul, don't hold it."

Read the Contents

Ryan was going through the process of decluttering his vehicle and asked these questions:

- How did this happen?

- When was it last used?

- Is this something that needs to be done back there?

- What if so?

- What will happen to my stuff if it's not put back there?

You can also ask about the contents of your cabinets, house, or even your desktop computer. You can also ask for information about the activities you do not enjoy and the people you share your time with. It allows you to prioritise things and activities that add value to you life, and lets go of negative people and activities that don't serve you well.

Reduce, Reuse and Recycle

Once you have decluttered your life's physical spaces, you can make a conscious decision to stop cluttering again. Reduce your clutter and reduce your purchases. Keep your purchases to a minimum. Purchase only what you absolutely need. No matter if you're buying them in bulk or retail pieces, don't purchase things just because they're cheap. By buying fewer items, your possessions can be reused, repurposed, and recycled. Here's another tip...

Spend only on essentials

Some people make bold moves to break the cycle of consumerism and live a more frugal lifestyle. There are many people who have taken a consumer fast: Assya Barre's 200 day ban on buying new items, Michelle McGagh's 6 months of doing nothing, Rosamund Linnin's 30 days without spending anything, and Michelle McGagh's 6 month long ban on spending new things.

This recipe and its variations are also available.

Don't spend more than you need on things like shampoo, toothpaste, shampoo and soap. You should also consider moisturizer and deodorant essentials. Your body is the best source of information about your hygiene. Pay attention to it. It's possible to try not using moisturizer or any deodorant for one or two days and then see if you feel the need.

Do not shop around. Purchase only the basic necessities of life: basic food and basic toiletries. Don't eat out or purchase prepared food. Instead, cook at home and share the meal with your family. Instead of going to the movies, instead watch a film or series at home. You can stream a lot of movies online. Instead of purchasing gifts for occasions, why don't you create something like a personalized ref magnet, knitted scarfs, poetry, or even a soothing massage?

Instead of driving your car, you should ride a bicycle. If you don't know the basics of biking, you can learn. Public transportation is an option if you can't bike. You should gauge it according to your daily activities. For example, if you are attending a client's meeting, you might choose to drive, take a ride or hail a taxi to get to the meeting.

It's important to not spend too much on unnecessary stuff and to find other ways. This will allow you to see that you don't always require money to enjoy life. Energy and time are two other resources you can use.

If you find the concept of engaging consumers quickly too overwhelming or bold, then start small. You can just reduce your consumer spending.

Joshua Becker suggests asking questions before buying or purchasing anything. It doesn't matter if you are buying a new garment, a new piece furniture, or a pet. Erika Bragdon, a blogger mom, gives a summary of the questions we need.

7 Things to Consider before You Buy Something

1. Is there a reason for this item?

2. How long can this item last for?

3. How often do I actually use this?

4. Can this create chaos and clutter?

5. It's why am I considering buying it? Do I want it because a close friend has it or to be told? Do I want to purchase it to satisfy an empty feeling? Do I want to show the salesperson that I can buy it? Do I want to impress others or work colleagues with my purchase?

6. Do I have the right to buy this product today?

7. Is there any other option to this purchase?

Figure 11: 7 Reasons for Buying by Erika Brangdon

I know of a young lady, who spent a whole year paying off credit card debt. After paying off her debt she decided to be more careful with how she spent her money. When she finds something she likes at a department store she won't immediately buy it. She sleeps on it. It's not something she returns to often.

She also learned how to wrap her credit card in tape-sealed tissue paper, which helped her be more mindful about using it. By doing so, she only opens the paper when she really needs it.

An older lady was the one who taught her daughters to use credit cards effectively. She would always remind them that credit cards were not the same as cash. Treating your credit cards as cash would only make you more debt. Make sure you use it wisely. It is important to use it wisely.

It's making purpose-driven, informed purchases instead of buying impulse items that you will regret later or feel buyer's remorse.

Rethink your attachments

Do you really need a huge house? What if you could live in a smaller space? What if the move is to your parents' home or with your sibling?

Are you really in need of a sports car? What if you buy a smaller car or a motorcycle instead? Do you really need a gasoline-powered vehicle? What if your only purpose was to ride a bicycle or walk more?

Do you really need expensive jewelries, luxury cars, and real estate? Society tells us that these are good investments.

Do you really need to subscribe to grocery delivery and gym memberships? Do you have to try every restaurant that opens? Do you need a loyalty certificate for all retail and restaurant establishments?

Let's now look at start ups. Hamish McRae noticed and pointed out that Uber, which is the largest taxi service in the world, does not own any cars. Facebook, the world's largest media company, has no content. Alibaba, the world's most valued retailer, doesn't own any stock. Airbnb, the largest hotel provider in the world, has no stock. It's a big deal.

It is possible to shift the paradigm of business models. You can also change your attitude and see attachment as a way to redefine possession. Consider your life without a specific possession. Now think of ways that you can live your life with no particular item. You might be pleasantly surprised by the ideas and alternatives that you come up with.

Manage your Digital and Online Life

Organize your digital life. It may be helpful to clean up your files. Make sub-folders or folders according to your needs. You can for example separate your business folders or files from your personal files.

Arrange photos according dates, years, or events. Instead of storing all your stuff in one big folder, collect all your ebooks in one folder.

You can do the same thing on your mobile devices. It will be easier for users to locate your files and apps if they are organized in a way that makes it easier.

It may also be beneficial to review your online habits and implement minimalism. Unsubscribe from email subscribers. You can do this manually, or you can use unroll online for free.

Unfollow accounts and pages from social media. Social media contacts who post mostly negative status updates, or other contents that are stressful to you should be unfriended. Your life will change if your social media account is deactivated for days or even weeks. Deactivate your social media accounts and other online forums/sites that you don't use often or do not benefit you.

To convert paper mails, such as utility bills and bank statements, to password-protected statements for billing, you can opt to send them to your email. This will help you save on paper and make it easier to manage your bills.

Eat only the Essentials, Move More

Minimalism can be beneficial for your health. It encourages you and others to focus on nutrition and taking good care of your body.

Intermittent fasting (a popular idea and practice these days) is one way. Intermittent fasting allows you to eat less and frees up time for other activities. It can also address yoyo dieting and help people to lose weight.

There are many variations on this diet. However, the basic principle is that there should be a period where you eat followed by a period when you fast. Some people eat one time per day, while others eat four to 10 hours a day. This makes the body burn stored fats, rather than consume fats, and increases its fasting period.

Learn more about this practice through blogs and online articles. You can also decide to give it a try to see if you like it.

Intermittent fasting may not be for you. Minimalism can also be good for your health. You can experiment with organic eating, vegetarianism, and other forms of minimalism.

You don't need to be a vegetarian, an intermittent faster, or organic eater. It's as easy as mindful eating. This means choosing foods that nourish the body rather than harming it.

You don't need to be a yogi. It could be as simple as moving more than you sit all day or adding movement to your daily routine. You can walk your dog together or go for a stroll through the park with your partner instead of spending hours scrolling through Facebook or television.

If you are interested in yoga or vegetarianism, you can practice them. However, you will not be better or worse for doing this or that. Do what you can, and then let go of the rest.

You should create a budget, and then stick to it

A second benefit to minimalism? Financial management. If you prioritise your life, your money will go where your heart is. You should not spend your money on frivolous things or on things that aren't adding value to your lives, or on items that don't serve your heart or your intentions.

You should prioritize your priorities when creating your budget. This is how budgets are allocated by some people monthly and yearly. This example is not meant to be a limitation. Budget prioritization will vary from person to person. This is a rough example to illustrate budget allocation. This budget can be adapted to fit your lifestyle and priorities.

- 50% Daily Essentials and Necessities

- 20% Nutrition (groceries)

- 10% Lodging (rental or mortgage)

- 10% Mobility for fuel and transportation

- 10% Miscellaneous

Get 10% off

- 10% Deposit

- 10% Self-improvement with books, courses and seminars

10% Rest and recreation to nourish your spirit

- 10% Give it back (donations to charities, churches, and causes)

Figure 12: A sample budget allocation (single person living independently)

Identify your current position, priorities, as well as future plans. Budget allocations for one person might be different than those of married couples with 5 children. A backpacker traveler might have a different budget to a business owner.

www.ingramcontent.com/pod-product-compliance
Lightning Source LLC
Chambersburg PA
CBHW050402120526
44590CB00015B/1797